EXECUTIVE CLEMENCY BY PARDON:

A GUIDE TO PARDON SUCCESS

SIMONE R. RICHARDSON

iUNIVERSE, INC.
BLOOMINGTON

Executive Clemency by Pardon: A Guide to Pardon Success

iUniverse books may be ordered through booksellers or by contacting:

iUniverse
1663 Liberty Drive
Bloomington, IN 47403
www.iuniverse.com
1-800-Authors (1-800-288-4677)

Because of the dynamic nature of the Internet, any Web addresses or links contained in this book may have changed since publication and may no longer be valid. The views expressed in this work are solely those of the author and do not necessarily reflect the views of the publisher, and the publisher hereby disclaims any responsibility for them.

ISBN: 978-1-4502-6592-8 (sc)
ISBN: 978-1-4502-6593-5 (ebk)

Library of Congress Control Number: 2010917406

Printed in the United States of America

iUniverse rev. date: 8/25/2011

DEDICATION

To the formerly incarcerated people and ex-offenders
who are striving to live a productive crime free life.

My Zen

We are all interconnected.
The ex-offender's stress is my stress.
The ex-offender's pain is my pain.
Whatever burdens the ex-offender will eventually burden me.
Whatever worries the ex-offender will eventually worry me.
Whatever affects one will eventually affect the other.
As I heal the pain and suffering of the ex-offender,
I heal the pain and suffering in me.

Simone R. Richardson

CONTENTS

PREFACE

What I learned through my experience meeting ex-offenders as a public library librarian helped me acquire deep understanding, wisdom, and compassion, concerning the plight of the formerly incarcerated person. In addition, I acquired a deep understanding through my ex-offender related research, facilitation of library job search workshops, past resume seminars, and volunteer work with the homeless and formerly incarcerated persons. As a result of my research and compassion, I composed *Executive Clemency by Pardon: A Guide to Pardon Success.*

Executive Clemency by Pardon: A Guide to Pardon Success may be useful for the official or teacher who assists the ex-offender. The resource is also geared toward the ex-offender (formerly incarcerated or not) who obtained the mental strength, determination, and acquired the education to turn his or her life around for the betterment of society. The resource targets the individual who decides to take on the additional challenge; the challenge to apply for a pardon.

Executive Clemency by Pardon is a helpful guide for the former offender who can express, as a narrative on a pardon application, atonement for the mistakes of the past. The resource may benefit the applicant who can accept responsibility for wrongdoing and convey eagerness to right the harm done to others. The guide may encourage the former offender to develop and provide the evidence (on the pardon application) of giving back to the community that which was taken during the committing of the crime.

The pardon application process is a long one and acquiring a pardon is not guaranteed. The applicant's life may be thoroughly investigated by pardon officials, and the pardon may not be granted the first time around. The wait for results may take some time, and the gathering of necessary documents is a tedious task. The applicant must make professional friends or acquaintances because those friends will be needed to write letters of support and recommendation. If a pardon hearing is granted, the applicant is interviewed in front of members of the pardon board. Also, other people will attend the pardon hearing who may be in support or against the applicant.

A pardon denial should not be an excuse for the former offender to fail to achieve or fail to accomplish a goal. The pardon applicant must continue to strive to obtain training, education, or volunteer experience. The applicant must continue to set a positive example and make a difference in the community. It must be understood that, as the Honorable M. Michael Rounds, Governor of South Dakota said, "No inmate, regardless of the offense, is entitled to parole or a pardon; they are rewards that must be earned and merited."

Allow the tips in this resource to be the path to the reward. Take the advice in this guide to gain the necessary merit.

Simone R. Richardson

Acknowledgements

Special thanks to:

The United States Pardon Attorneys Roger C. Adams and the current one Ronald L. Rodgers; the Honorable M. Michael Rounds, Governor of South Dakota; Roni Burkes, Administrative Assistant, and JoEllen Culp, Public Affairs Liaison of the Ohio Department of Rehabilitation and Correction; C.A. Crofts, counsel to Governor Freudenthal of Wyoming; the Honorable Dave Freudenthal, Governor of Wyoming; Kent Wm. Jones, Senior Hearing Officer for the Utah Board of Pardons and Parole; the Honorable John Elias Baldacci, Governor of Maine; Maine Board of Executive Clemency; Rita Menard, Assistant to Executive Counsel of Rhode Island; and M. Campbell, Legal Affairs Coordinator for the state of Washington.

Additional Thanks go to:

Audrey Blodgett, Paralegal, Attorney General of New Hampshire; Judy Leavitt, Pardon Clerk, Maine Secretary of State; Mindy Dumermuth, Wisconsin Deputy Legal Counsel; and Karla Black, Maine Deputy Legal Counsel.

I'm deeply appreciative to all the other state officials who mailed me a copy of their state pardon applications and instructions, made those applications available on the state Web sites, or sent the information to me via email.

Simone R. Richardson

Visit Simone's Web site:

http://zenclemency.tripod.com

Note: The governors and Web sites listed in this resource may be different by the time of publication.

INTRODUCTION

There is no guarantee a pardon will be granted. The steps taken by the applicant to prepare for the pardon, however, will not only help the individual seeking the pardon live a better life and help the people surrounding the seeker; the steps will benefit the entire world.

Executive Clemency by Pardon: A Guide to Pardon Success provides tips to enhance an ex-offender's chances for being considered for the presidential or state pardon. According to the resource, pardon officials not only look for applicants who live a crime free life but officials look for the following:

1. The applicant's participation in the community:
   • Volunteering
   • Involvement in charity
   • Community service
2. The nature and seriousness of the crime.
3. Educational and employment pursuits.
4. Accomplishments and achievements of the applicant.

Living a better life, however, is dependent on the ex-offender making rehabilitative decisions in the form of exemplary conduct. There are many examples of exemplary conduct.

Executive Clemency by Pardon will focus on the conduct of finding employment, volunteering for an organization that helps others, creating a volunteer project that helps others, and receiving an education and career to inspire fellow ex-offenders. The pardon guide provides tips and resources on how to achieve each exemplary conduct discussed.

Executive Clemency by Pardon: A Guide to Pardon Success also reveals examples from actual state pardon applications so that readers may discover the differences between, and analyze the characteristics of, state pardon applications granted versus state pardon applications denied. In addition, brief state-by-state pardon contact and eligibility information is included to help the former offender get started with the pardon process.

The pardon is referred to as executive clemency.

CHAPTER 1

WHAT IS EXECUTIVE CLEMENCY?

A pardon is part of an umbrella term called executive clemency. Executive clemency is the constitutional power of the governor or president to issue a commutation of sentence, pardon, and reprieve.

COMMUTATION

The commutation is the shortening of a punishment to one less harsh. It is the reduction of a sentence. The commutation, for instance, is a request to be released from incarceration by way of being eligible for parole at an earlier date.

PARDON

The pardon is not an expungement or sealing of a conviction but represents forgiveness of punishment and guilt. It is preferred that a candidate for pardon have many years of living crime free. The pardon restores rights lost as a result of the criminal conviction.

REPRIEVE

The reprieve usually applies to individuals on death-row. The reprieve request delays the carrying out of the sentence.

A Pardon is not an Expungement

Before discussing the pardon (presidential and state), the expungement must be defined. An expungement means that a conviction is removed from a person's record. No one has access to a record once it is expunged. For instance, once a record is expunged in juvenile court the record is erased forever. Expungement law varies from state to state. An expungement, in Ohio law, is the process of "sealing" a criminal record.

Sealed records may still be accessed in situations in which an individual commits a future crime. In other words, a sealed record may be used against an individual in sentencing. Probation and law enforcement personnel may access sealed records if a person decides to work with children, work with older citizens, or decides to strive for a career as a police officer. An expungement in Ohio is only granted to an individual with one conviction. An expungement in Ohio is also not granted to those convicted of the following crimes: a sexual crime, a first-degree violent misdemeanor, a mandatory prison term, a first or second degree felony, a first degree misdemeanor, or a felony in which the victim is under 18. Also, an individual's record will not be sealed if other criminal charges are outstanding.

Timeframe in Ohio

The time period for applying for an expungement is one year after time served for a misdemeanor, and three years after time served for a felony.

Expungement Procedure

The procedure for expungement is simple in Ohio. In the county where the crime occurred, request the final order from the court. Also, request the "Motion for Sealing of Criminal Record" forms. After completing the forms, notarized the affidavit and file the forms with the clerk of courts.

The final steps in the expungement process include a meeting in the probation department, a court hearing set by the judge, and a filing fee. An Affidavit of Indigency or poverty affidavit may be requested and filed for those who are unable to pay the filing fee. For more information

on expungement law in Ohio consult the Ohio Revised Code Ann. §
2953.31 and Ohio Revised Code Ann. § 2953.32.

Remember, the expungement process may vary from state to state.
Contact the clerk of courts office in the county where the crime occurred
to find out the local expungement law and procedure.

WHAT IS PRESIDENTIAL PARDON?

A presidential pardon (Article II, Section 2, and Clause 1 of the
Constitution) is not an indication or restoration of a person's innocence.
In addition, the presidential pardon does not erase or expunge a criminal
conviction. The idea of a presidential pardon "not" erasing or expunging
a conviction (state or federal) is emphasized in a letter I received from
the office of the United States pardon attorney. The letter is a response to
my inquiry, dated May 29, 2007, concerning information about federal
pardons. The third paragraph of the attorney's correspondence reads:

> For your information, a presidential pardon for a
> federal conviction does not erase or expunge the judicial
> records of a conviction, and I know of no federal
> statutory procedure to expunge an adult conviction.
> Expungement, to the extent available, is a judicial
> remedy and it is rarely granted. However, a pardon will
> facilitate removal of legal disabilities imposed because
> of the conviction, and should lessen to some extent
> the stigma arising from the conviction. In addition, a
> pardon may be helpful in obtaining license, bonding, or
> employment. Additionally, I would suggest that anyone
> who is trying to have their state conviction expunged
> contact their Governor or other state authorities because
> it is our understanding that the states have different
> procedures for 'expunging' a conviction or 'clearing'
> the record of a criminal conviction for violation of state
> law.

*Reprinted by permission from the Office of the Pardon Attorney, U.S.
Department of Justice, 2007. The above paragraph, being a government
document and in public domain, is not subjected to copyright status in this
publication.*

A pardon recipient must still reveal a conviction when asked on an application. The positive aspect of revealing a criminal past on an application is that evidence of a pardon may also be included.

Remember, a presidential pardon relieves the prejudice and mark of shame surrounding a criminal record and takes away legal constraints and other ramifications shadowing a past conviction. The pardon also improves an individual's chances of obtaining a license for jobs that were denied the pardon recipient after his or her conviction.

The presidential pardon is a form of forgiveness of a crime dependent upon the applicant taking responsibility for his or her actions, revealing atonement or remorse in some way, and living crime free for a period of time after release from incarceration or the ending of a sentence.

Presidential pardons are given to individuals who commit federal crimes. Only the president of the United States grants presidential pardons.

Some examples of federal crimes include the following:

Bank Robberies	Insurance Fraud
Bankruptcy Fraud	Jewelry and Gem Theft
Cargo Theft	Money Laundering
Hate Crime	Mortgage Fraud
Identity Theft	Telemarketing Fraud

Source: FBI "What We Investigate." www.fbi.gov/hq.htm.

To review or acquire the record of a federal conviction, contact the clerk of federal courts in the city where the crime occurred.

To begin the presidential executive clemency process by pardon, first request an application or petition (as it is also called) from the pardon attorney's office:

Office of the Pardon Attorney
U.S. Department of Justice
1425 New York Avenue N.W.
Washington, DC 20530-0001
202.616.6070

Pardon applications and information about the presidential pardon procedure may also be acquired from the pardon attorney's Web site: http://www.usdoj.gov/pardon.

Before considering and submitting an application for presidential pardon, applicants must wait five years after the date of release from incarceration. If the result of a conviction is no prison or jail time (a fine or probation for example) applicants must wait five years starting on the date of sentencing. Any supervised release, parole or probation, must be finalized before submitting an application for presidential pardon. Individuals who have military convictions may request an application from the pardon attorney but should submit the application directly to the secretary of the military department that orchestrated the court-martial trial.

An applicant must provide and describe the most recent federal conviction on the pardon application. All other federal crimes must also be provided and described but as part of an attachment to the application. Any additional arrests, civil lawsuits, and credit delinquencies are also required as part of the pardon application.

The seeker of a federal pardon should state, in detail, why the pardon is desired. To strengthen the request, the seeker should include additional evidence and documentation to help in the enhancement of pardon consideration (letters from officials, licensing boards, and information from state statutes, regulations, or professional associations, for example).

Pardon representatives analyze, extensively, information provided on a pardon application. For instance, an official from the U.S. government may interview people who filled out a reference or "character affidavit" on behalf of the applicant. The character affidavit describes positive qualities, attributes, and other character uplifting information about the pardon seeker. The presidential pardon application provides three character affidavits. Pardon officials may also interview current and past employers.

PRESIDENTIAL PARDON OFFICIALS' CRITERIA

The characteristics presidential pardon officials look for in an application include the following:

1. The pardon seeker's participation in the community.
2. The seeker's activities related to charity.
3. The seriousness of the crime.

4. The criminal history of the applicant.
5. The misfortune experienced by the applicant because of the federal crime.

If an individual is denied a presidential pardon a two year wait, starting on the date of the denial, is required before a person may submit a new application.

Applications for pardon must be thoroughly and truthfully filled out in ink or typed. According to information obtained from the office of the pardon attorney, five years imprisonment will be imposed on applicants who provide false information. Individuals who include false information may also expect a fine of $250, 000.

STATE PARDON OFFICIALS' CRITERIA

In response to my inquiry posed to state governors and pardon board officials concerning the factors that are considered in a pardon application when granting a pardon, I asked the following question:

> What three factors, characteristics, or qualities about an individual's pardon application prompts or encourages you to grant him or her a pardon?

C.A. Crofts who is counsel to Dave Freudenthal, governor of Wyoming, responded in the following way:

> I can say that in general Governor Freudenthal will not even consider an application for a pardon until ten years have passed since the completion of sentence, to include probation or parole. He expects that ten year period to be free from any crimes or other legal difficulties. It also depends on the nature of the crime, and he generally will not consider a pardon for crimes against children, for example. People who have committed crimes of violence are less likely to be pardoned than 'white collar' criminals, I suppose, but that is not an absolute rule. He gives strong credence to the wishes of the victims, or victims' families. He will look at whether or not restitution has been made. And he looks at the

subsequent life history of the applicant. Generally he expects some significant affirmative contribution to the life of the community, or improvement in the life of the applicant, such as attaining college or training—not just the mere managing to escape further difficulty with the law for ten years. In other words, he expects an affirmative demonstration of rehabilitation and improved character. He grants pardons fairly rarely, and does not consider this to be a pro forma right that is granted simply upon completion of the sentence that was imposed by the court.

From the office of the Honorable Dave Freudenthal, Governor of Wyoming, June 26, 2008. Correspondence by C.A. Crofts, counsel to the governor. Reprinted by permission.

The Utah Board of Pardons & Parole which has the sole authority to grant full and unconditional pardons in Utah analyzes the candidate's crime:

When we conduct a hearing, we consider all aspects of the applicant's crime, including aggravating and mitigating circumstances, both present and past. The five Board Members have the final determination in all matters. As you have accurately pointed out, some entities of society stigmatize former inmates, although they have paid their debt to society. Such a pardon may assist to restore their rights.

From the office of the Utah Board of Pardons & Parole, September 18, 2008. Correspondence by Kent Wm. Jones, Senior Hearing Officer. Reprinted by permission.

The state of Maine Governor's Board of Executive Clemency provided the following advice:

The Governor has established the Governor's Board of Executive Clemency to assist him with reviewing and making recommendation on applications for executive clemency. In order to be considered for a pardon, an individual must demonstrate a compelling and appropriate need for clemency. The Governor's Board of Executive Clemency considers a number of factors when weighing an applicant's petition for a pardon, including, but not limited to: (1) whether an applicant's conviction has limited his or her employment opportunities; (2) whether an applicant accepts responsibility for his or her actions; (3) whether an applicant is remorseful for those actions; and (4) whether the applicant has taken steps to turn his or her life around.

From the office of the Honorable John Elias Baldacci, Governor of Maine, October 29, 2008. Correspondence by Karla Black, Deputy Legal Counsel. Reprinted by permission.

M. Michael Rounds, governor of South Dakota, offered suggestions in his own words:

First and foremost, my belief is no inmate, regardless of the offense, is entitled to parole or a pardon; they are rewards that must be earned and merited. Secondly, I consider the possibility and likelihood the offender will turn his or her life around and become a valued member of the community, and contribute to society in a positive manner. Lastly, I weigh the chances he or she would re-offend, harm others, and end up back in the corrections system.

In South Dakota, the Board of Pardons and Paroles conducts preliminary investigations into requests from inmates and sends a recommendation to me for final consideration. I study each report thoroughly and make my decision based on the facts at hand, and I don't always agree with the board's recommendation.

I consider this to be one of the most important duties of any governor; to balance the desire of an offender who may truly want to improve his or her life, with the greater good and safety of the population as a whole.

From the office of the Honorable M. Michael Rounds, Governor of South Dakota, November 5, 2008. Reprinted by permission.

Iowa Governor's Legal Department

In a phone conversation I had with the Iowa Governor's Legal Department, which is comprised of the Governor's General Counsel, the department provided the following recommendations to help applicants with pardon success:

1. Although the pardon application doesn't require this information, it is important to include letters of recommendation from the following:
    *   Prosecuting Attorney
    *   Sentencing Judge
    *   Local Sheriff
    *   Employers
2. The Iowa Legal Department encourages applicants to follow closely the instructions in the pardon application.
3. The governor will look at the nature of the offense and the criminal history of the applicant.
4. The governor likes to see at least 10 years of crime free living before an application is considered. The governor may also consider an applicant with less time. It depends on the contents of the application.
5. The contents of the application include the investigation of the applicant's background (personal contacts and employer interviews) which also plays a role in the pardon consideration. Pardon officials may also interview the applicant.
6. When considering the content of the application, the Iowa Legal Department recommends that the applicant "paints the full picture" of his or her life in an application, including information that highlights what the applicant has done over time.

CHAPTER 2

FINDING EMPLOYMENT

EXAMPLES OF EXEMPLARY CONDUCT

One important request seen on some state pardon applications is evidence of outstanding conduct (what good deeds has one accomplished since the ending of the sentence). Throughout this book, I'm going to call such request "evidence of exemplary conduct." Chapter 9 reveals the exemplary conduct request on some state pardon applications.

The following chapters will provide resources, examples, and tips on achieving the exemplary conduct of finding employment, volunteering one's time, creating a volunteer project, and pursuing an education and career.

FINDING EMPLOYMENT: THE INFORMATIONAL INTERVIEW

One reason to strive for a pardon is for an opportunity to acquire quality employment—a better and higher paying job position. The pardon may also help a person gain employment license and bonding. It looks good, therefore, on a pardon application to reveal current employment (any employment). But first one has to find a job and what better way to get one's name out to potential employers than to talk to the employer directly—called the informational interview.

The informational interview is an important method (among many) to help job seekers promote their work experience and skills and network for jobs. The informational interview is important because some employers do not advertise job openings. According to the DVD, *Starting Fresh: Finding a Job with a Troubled Background*, about 80 percent of job positions are never seen in newspaper ads or online employment sites. Also, some employers don't advertise publicly because they find workers through other means like referrals, recommendations from other employees, contacting people directly, or through recruiters.

INFORMATIONAL INTERVIEW INSTRUCTIONS

1. Make a list of companies to work for (your skills and experience should match the company's job requirements).
2. Research the background of each company.
3. Call each company one by one and ask for the manager or director or the head of human resources (talk to the person who does the hiring).

   > Note: For a list of company phone numbers check your local phone book or contact the business and government section of your local library.

4. For instance, when addressing a company one could say the following:

   > Good morning, my name is Jane Friend; may I please speak to Ms. Smith the manager of the XYZ Company?

5. When the director or manager answers the phone you could respond:

   > Hello Ms. Smith, my name is Jane Friend. I'd like to have a brief discussion with you concerning your company. I'm especially interested in going into this business as a potential career. I'd like to ask you some brief questions about the job positions in this company and the_____ profession as a whole.

6. Schedule a time and date to interview the employer. In this reverse interview you are the interviewer.

7. Once a date to meet is scheduled, dress professionally for the interview and arrive on time.

8. When you meet the director/manager introduce yourself and shake the employer's hand. Next, interview the employer. The interview may go something similar to the following:

INTERVIEW THE EMPLOYER

1. Ms. Smith, could you describe your typical day?
2. What are your most important responsibilities?
3. What made you go into this profession?
4. What are the challenges facing this profession?
5. What educational requirements would be helpful for the positions in this company?
6. What qualities would help a person succeed in this environment?
7. What do you expect out of the employees who work here?
8. What goals do you see this company achieving in the next five years?
9. How do you encourage employees to achieve the goals of the company?
10. Ms. Smith, could you direct me to other professionals who have expertise in this industry?

9. Keep a copy of your resume and references ready. The references should be typed and on a page separate from your resume. The employer may discuss your skills and experience at the interview.

10. If you happen to receive a referral from another industry leader, set up a meeting and interview the new employer as well.

11. When the interview is complete thank the employer and shake hands again. Type and mail the employer a thank you note for taking time out to talk with you.

The informational interview is the technique of networking for potential job leads. The job search may be stressful but never give up. Perseverance is the key. Even if an entry level job, a seasonal job, or a temporary job is found, the job will provide work experience and will look good on a pardon application.

The informational interview is called a nontraditional job search method. Traditional job search methods include newspaper classified ads, applying directly to the company (online or in person), or calling a company to inquire about a position. Additional job search methods include job fairs, employment agencies, temporary services, visiting the local One-Stop job center (www.careeronestop.org), and consulting nonprofit and faith-based organizations that help ex-offenders find employment. Try each and every job search method until a position is found. Never give up!

Also, your local library's business and government division will provide online as well as print job search resources.

For more tips on job searching check out the following DVDs: *Starting Fresh: Finding a Job with a Troubled Background; Starting Fresh: Interviewing with a Troubled Background;* and *Starting Fresh: Resumes & Cover Letters with a Troubled Background,* by Linx Educational copyright 2007.

FORMULATING THE RESUME FOR EMPLOYMENT

Work experience obtained in prison is worthy experience to add to the resume. One example of worthy experience is prison community service. For instance, according to the Ohio Department of Rehabilitation and Correction, the department incorporates prison community service into its programs:

> Community Service supports a variety of partnerships including training and caring for puppies and dogs for programs that assist the physically and visually impaired; assisting Habitat for Humanity build homes for low to moderate income families; recording books on tape for schools; and serving approximately 200 teachers per day through Crayons to Computers, a free store for teachers. Since 1991, when the program was introduced, Department of Rehabilitation and Correction inmates have provided over 57 million community service hours to Ohio's Communities.

The formerly incarcerated individual's resume may reflect the community partnerships between the prison and a nonprofit organization. For instance, incarcerated individuals play a significant role in home building for Habitat for Humanity (www.habatat.org) according to the Ohio DRC. Let's say that an incarcerated individual wants to work as a construction laborer when he or she is released from prison. The resume must reflect construction related activity. When formulating the resume, prison volunteer experience from the Habitat organization may be written in the following way:

1. First, the nonprofit organization may be listed as the employer:
   Habitat for Humanity

2. Next, the position worked is listed:
   Laborer or Construction Laborer

3. Work duties are included using bullet points starting with the action verbs **constructed**, **installed**, and **painted**. For instance, the former offended could write the following:
   - Constructed staircases, bathroom and kitchen cabinets, pre-fabricated walls, and door and window frames.
   - Installed walls, wiring, plumbing, flooring, and siding and trusses.
   - Painted interior walls; hung drywall and assisted with exterior landscaping.

Note: According to the Ohio DRC, the above duties are the actual duties of inmates working on Habitat homes.

4. Let's fictionalize this resume a bit by including a "cause" and "effect" component to the resume. In other words, what did this resume writer do to make the job better? What are the results of the employment actions?

Action or Cause	Result or Effect
Constructed staircases, bathroom and kitchen cabinets, pre-fabricated walls, and door and window frames,	completing a one bedroom house in one month with a construction crew of 20 laborers.
Installed walls, wiring, plumbing, flooring, and siding and trusses,	completing 30 projects with little to no supervision and instruction from the project manager.
Painted interior walls; hung drywall and assisted with exterior landscaping,	maintaining a neat and safe working area for home occupiers and coworkers.

5. Let's also include that the incarcerated individual has experience using the following tools:

Equipment Operation

Power Drill; Rivet Gun; Blast Track Machine; Sand Muller; Power Screwdriver; Tow Motor; Jackhammer; Pallet Jack; Cement Mixer;

6. There may be other skills the fictional individual may want to include:

Skills
- Good attendance record
- Good manual speed and dexterity
- Highly motivated
- Fast learner

7. Additional work related skills acquired while incarcerated can also supplement the resume:

Additional Experience

Cook; Basic Computer; Data Entry; Dog Trainer; Baker; Floor Maintenance

The final resume may look similar to this resume.

John Doe

123 Main Avenue
Akron, Ohio 44320
330-123-4567
jdoe@emailaddress.com

Work Experience

2006-2009
Habitat for Humanity   **Akron, Ohio**
Construction Laborer

- Constructed staircases, bathroom and kitchen cabinets, pre-fabricated walls, and door and window frames, completing a two bedroom house in one month with a construction crew of 20 laborers.

- Installed walls, wiring, plumbing, flooring, and siding and trusses, completing 30 projects with little to no supervision and instruction from the project manager.

- Painted interior walls; hung drywall and assisted with exterior landscaping, maintaining a neat and safe working area for home occupiers and coworkers.

Equipment Operation

Power Drill ◆ Rivet Gun ◆ Blast Track Machine ◆ Sand Muller ◆ Power Screwdriver ◆ Tow Motor ◆ Jackhammer ◆ Pallet Jack ◆ Cement Mixers

Skills

Good attendance record ◆ Good manual speed and dexterity ◆ Highly motivated ◆ Fast learner

Additional Experience

Cook; Basic Computer; Data Entry; Dog Trainer; Baker; Floor Maintenance

CHAPTER 3

VOLUNTEER YOUR TIME

Volunteer activity looks good on a pardon application. Volunteering is not only good work experience but an individual can network with other people thereby discovering leads to potential jobs. The volunteer activity may include working at the local soup kitchen, helping the homeless, or teaching adults how to read and write. Volunteer choices in America are limitless. There are volunteer opportunities in almost every community in the United States. The following organizations and Web sites may provide volunteer ideas and connections to organizations. Also, the local newspaper or religious center (church, synagogue, or temple) may have additional volunteering ideas or opportunities. Many nonprofit organizations work on a limited budget and may welcome volunteers.

HABITAT FOR HUMANITY
www.habatat.org

One organization to volunteer for is Habitat for Humanity. Habitat for Humanity is a Christian housing ministry with the goal to eliminate homelessness and poverty due to the loss or lack of shelter. Habitat for Humanity constructs and rehabilitates basic homes for low income families. The Habitat homes are not free. Home owners are required to help in the construction of their homes. After a small down payment there is a mortgage to pay.

Habitat offices are located throughout the United States and various locations around the world including Africa, the Middle East, Asia and Pacific, and Europe and Central Asia. To locate a Habitat for Humanity organization, search by state, country, affiliate name or zip code on the organization's Web site. Write to Habitat at the following address:

Habitat for Humanity
121 Habitat Street
Americus, Georgia 31709-3498
800-422-4828

Martin Luther King Jr. Day of Service
www.mlkday.gov

Coordinate and organize a community volunteer activity with help and advice from the Martin Luther King Jr. Day of Service Toolkit. Find the kit by clicking on "MLK Day Mobilization tools and tips" at the bottom left side of the Web site. According to the toolkit, in 1994, Congress passed the King Holiday and Service Act which celebrated King's legacy of social change through community service.

Martin Luther King Jr. Day is not a day of rest but a day of volunteer work. It is through work that people build better communities, show compassion toward each other, and interact with people of different faiths, ethnic backgrounds, and races.

The MLK Day of Service is supported by the Corporation for National and Community Service which is a federal agency developed with the goal of enhancing communities through service.

The toolkit recommends that participants partner with local community organizations. The kit also provides a step-by-step guide on how to publicize to the public, organize volunteers, and properly plan a community project. Project ideas from the toolkit include serving meals to the homeless, cleaning up vandalism from buildings, planting trees and flowers in the community, and building playgrounds to name a few.

SERVE.GOV
www.serve.gov

Serve.gov is a site designed not only to help people find volunteer opportunities in their area but designed to encourage people to create their own volunteer project. Serve.gov is the Web site of a national initiative called United We Serve. Spearheaded by President Obama and the First Lady, Serve.gov encourages all Americans, no matter their race, ethnicity, or religious affiliation, to make service to the community a part of their daily lives.

Becoming a part of United We Serve is simple. Once an account is created on the site, visitors can register a project and invite other volunteers to join. If visitors are not sure how to get started on a project, Serve.gov provides toolkits for guidance.

UNITED WAY
http://liveunited.org

The United Way, the nation's largest charity, has a volunteer center. To find a local United Way agency, and to view current volunteer opportunities in an area, simply enter a zip code at the top right corner of the Web site. According to the organization, some benefits to volunteering include gaining work experience, learning new skills, enhancing a resume, and networking. Volunteer for a United Way agency and one criteria pardon officials look for in an application will be satisfied: involvement in charity.

CHAPTER 4

EDUCATIONAL AND CAREER ENDEAVORS

CAREER ENDEAVORS

Before venturing into an education, an individual must know what career to go into. The following resources provide descriptions and earnings for a cornucopia of careers.

BEST JOBS FOR EX-OFFENDERS

Careers open to formerly incarcerated persons are found in *Best Jobs for Ex-Offenders* by Ron Krannich. *Best Jobs* describes and targets 101 jobs in 13 occupation categories. *Best Jobs* not only list potential careers for ex-inmates but discusses the education, training, and qualifications connected to those careers.

ENCYCLOPEDIA OF CAREERS AND VOCATIONAL GUIDANCE

The *Encyclopedia of Careers and Vocational Guidance* list over 700 careers in over 90 industries and includes information on resume writing, cover letters, and interviewing skills. In addition, the encyclopedia provides readers with advice on selecting a career with help from assessment tests. The resource includes information on job searching including networking, job fairs, classified ads, and job placement offices.

The encyclopedia describes the background, structure, and outlook of the occupation. There is also a section for additional information.

OCCUPATIONAL OUTLOOK HANDBOOK
www.bls.gov/OCO/

The *Occupational Outlook Handbook* highlights occupations by describing the nature of the work, employment information, the job outlook, earnings, training, and other qualifications.

The handbook describes occupations and includes information on applying for jobs, lists the fastest growing occupations, and includes sources for training and financial aid.

Using employment projections from the U.S. Bureau of Labor Statistics, the *Occupational Outlook Handbook* is the U.S. government's primary occupation reference resource. The publication has been in existence since 1940.

ONET DICTIONARY OF OCCUPATIONAL TITLES
http://online.onetcenter.org

The *ONET Dictionary of Occupational Titles,* created by the U.S. Department of Labor, lists more than 950 job descriptions. ONET stands for Occupational Information Network. The resource showcases occupations by including the following: the training required, salary information, duties of the job, values necessary, required skills, the personality type helpful for the job, and the physical work conditions.

ONET occupations are given a number based on the federal governments numbering system called Standard Occupational Classification System (SOC). The SOC system classifies jobs according to the duties of the job. The ONET numbering system groups similar occupations together and lists them in numerical order.

EDUCATIONAL ENDEAVORS

The following resources will direct students to financial assistance for higher education and guide students to information on colleges and universities.

NATIONAL CENTER FOR EDUCATION STATISTICS COLLEGE NAVIGATOR

http://nces.ed.gov/collegenavigator

The National Center for Education Statistics maintains a College Navigator that can provide a guided college search that will help students look for the appropriate educational establishment. Find colleges in the Navigator by searching by name of school, state, zip code, award level (bachelor's or associate's), or by institution type (private or public; 2-year or 4-year).

STUDENTS.GOV

www.students.gov

A U.S. government Web site, Students.gov includes information about careers, scholarships, and financial assistance for school. The site also highlights various colleges and internships. Under the title "Campus life," there is a list of organizations that direct students to volunteer opportunities.

COLLEGE.GOV

www.college.gov

College.gov is a resource designed to help individuals with planning for higher education. Students will find assistance on preparing and paying for vocational schools, colleges, and universities. The college site is a one-stop-shop education resource compiled in one Web site. College. gov is developed by the U.S. Department of Education with assistance from students.

FAFSA4CASTER

www.fafsa4caster.ed.gov

FAFSA4caster is a place to start for students who are not quite ready to enter higher education and want additional information and guidance concerning financial aid.

FEDERAL STUDENT FINANCIAL AID
www.fafsa.ed.gov
1-800-433-3243.

When a student applies for federal student aid, he or she fills out a Free Application for Federal Student Aid (FAFSA). One question on the application asks if the applicant has ever been convicted of selling or possessing illegal drugs. After completing and mailing in the FAFSA, the student will receive the Student Aid Report (SAR). The Student Aid Report is a summary of the information reported on the FAFSA and reveals the amount of school money the student may receive.

What if the student answers "yes" to the drug conviction question on the FAFSA form?

If the student answers yes to the drug conviction question he or she will also receive the Student Aid Eligibility Worksheet for question 23 (question 23 is the illegal drug question number for the 2010-2011 school term, for instance). The Student Aid Eligibility Worksheet determines if the drug conviction affects the student's aid eligibility for the current school term.

There is a misconception that individuals with a felony drug conviction cannot receive federal student aid. A drug conviction will not stop a potential student from receiving federal school funding.

According to representatives at FAFSA, an individual may be denied federal student aid if the illegal drug offense occurred **during school enrollment** for which the student received federal aid. Also, even if a student is convicted for possessing or selling illegal drugs during the period of enrollment for which the student receives federal student aid, as long as the student completes a drug rehabilitation program since the conviction, the student is eligible for federal student aid. And, if the student is **not** eligible for federal student aid because of the conviction, he or she should still complete and send in the FAFSA because state or school financial aid may be available to the student.

For more information about federal financial assistance visit the FAFSA Web site:

- Go to www.fafsa.ed.gov.

- For questions concerning drug related convictions call the Federal Student Aid Information Center at 1-800-433-3243.
- Students may complete the FAFSA online or request the paper application form.

CHAPTER 5

FEDERAL EMPLOYMENT RESTRICTIONS

Remember, a pardon is not guaranteed. Bars to employment still exist legally, especially on a federal level. It is important to know which jobs are prohibited for certain felonies. The following employment areas include the corresponding federal laws related to employment restrictions.

CARE INVOLVING CHILDREN 42 USC § 13041

According to federal law, individuals seeking a job in child care services are to be subjected to a criminal background check. In addition, the law reads:

> Any conviction for a sex crime, an offense involving a child victim, or a drug felony, may be ground for denying employment or for dismissal of an employee... (42 USC § 13041c)

AIRPORT EMPLOYMENT 49 USC § 44936

Federal law requires criminal background checks for a person who considers a position as a security screener, or a position in which the person may have access to aircrafts and secured areas of an airport.

Individuals with certain felonies such as murder, treason, rape, armed robbery, and kidnapping (to name a few) are prohibited from this type of employment.

HEALTH CARE 42 USC § 1320A-7

Bars to employment (for certain felonies) exist for individuals considering jobs in health care programs in which Medicare is involved. A few examples include the following crimes:

- Abuse of patients
- Health care fraud
- Distribution or manufacture of a controlled substance

LABOR ORGANIZATIONS 29 USC § 504

An absolute bar to holding office is in place, for 13 years after a conviction or incarceration, in a labor organization (union) or organizations that handle employee benefits, for people who commit crimes such as robbery, arson, assault, rape, and extortion and other crimes listed in the federal law.

INSURANCE 18 USC § 1033

Bars to employment are in place in the insurance business unless the ex-offender acquires written permission from an insurance regulatory official.

BANKING INDUSTRY 12 USC § 1829

Employment in businesses insured by the FDIC or Federal Deposit Insurance Corporation is barred to individuals convicted of crimes of money laundering, dishonesty, and breach of trust. Waivers from the FDIC can be issued to restore employment for certain convictions. To review the FDIC regulations visit the following Web site:

www.fdic.gov/regulations/laws/rules/5000-1300.html.

PRISONER TRANSPORT 42 USC § 13726B

A person with a felony conviction or domestic violence conviction is barred from transporting prisoners. Also, criminal background checks and drug testing are required for individuals who apply for such employment.

ARMED FORCES

The military, in some cases, will issue conduct or moral waivers to those with questionable backgrounds. The U.S. Army's waiver information is found in AR (Army Regulation) 601-210 chapter 4. The Army also requires evidence of exemplary conduct by the applicant. Section 4-2(c) of the Army regulation requires the applicant to prove his or her worthiness:

> The burden is on the applicant to prove to waiver authorities that he or she has overcome their disqualifications for enlistment and that their acceptance would be in the best interests of the Army.

ADDITIONAL INFORMATION

For detailed descriptions of each federal employment restriction listed in this resource consult the Office of the Law Revision Counsel's Web site: http://uscode.house.gov. The Office of the Law Revision Counsel maintains and publishes the laws of the United States.

Chapter 6

Describing Evidence of Exemplary Conduct

Describing Atonement

The presidential pardon is the act of forgiving the crime in recognition of the applicant taking responsibility for his or her actions. The first step in taking responsibility for one's actions is the acknowledgement of wrongdoing and providing examples of atonement (giving back that which was taken away). For instance, at the section where the presidential pardon application says to give a "Reason for seeking pardon," one could provide a reason by beginning a paragraph with atonement similar to the following:

> A. I recognize that I hurt many people with my past actions including the victim (which I have made restitution). I have learned from my faults and have changed my attitude, actions, and ways for the better by (list positive ways you have changed your attitude and actions).

> B. I acknowledge that my past actions were counterproductive, and I'd like to present you with the many accomplishments I attained to try to

right the wrongs in my life (discuss, in detail, your accomplishments).

C. Although I cannot undo the past, I've changed my actions from actions that are harmful to ones that will make a better future for my community by (explain how you are making a better future for yourself and for the community).

D. There is no excuse for the poor decisions I made in the past and I take full responsibility for my crimes. Now, I have a new attitude and a new way of thinking, and I want to take the opportunity to give back to society that which I took away (discuss the many positive things you did to give back to society).

E. I acknowledge that I ruined lives and hurt many people by the crimes I committed. I acknowledge that there is no excuse for the poor decisions I made in the past. I ask for forgiveness for I am a changed person with a new way of acting and thinking. I present to you the evidence to prove my positive transformation (reveal the steps you took to better your life, to better your community, and to achieve your positive way of thinking).

Atonement may also be expressed on the state pardon application. In a few pardon applications, there is no evidence of the exemplary conduct request because there is no formal application to fill out. In other words, the applicant creates the application "package."

Living a crime free life is not enough. The governor and pardon board wants to see "how" one has lived a crime free life. For instance, pardon officials may want to know the following: Were your crime free years productive? Did you do something to help your fellow man or woman? Have you given back to society in some way?

In retrospect, remember the considerations presidential pardon officials look for in an application before a presidential pardon is considered:

1. The pardon seeker's participation in the community.
2. The seeker's activities related to charity.
3. The seriousness of the pardon seeker's crime.
4. The criminal history of the applicant.
5. The misfortune experienced by the applicant because of the federal crime.

In some states, it is the governor who decides whether to grant a clemency pardon after careful consideration and recommendation from the state board of pardons and parole. In other states, it is the sole authority of the board of pardons and parole to grant a pardon. And just like the characteristics for granting a presidential pardon, there are certain characteristics that a governor or state pardons board will look for in a pardon application.

After reading the chapters on the different types of exemplary conduct and after deciding which type of exemplary conduct to perform, how can an individual prove to pardon officials pardon worthiness? In retrospect, remember the evidence of exemplary conduct request found in the presidential pardon application:

> Describe any charitable or civic activities in which you have been engaged, or other contributions you have made to the community, since your conviction. In this regard you may include the names of any organizations in which you have participated, the time periods of your participation, your role in these activities, and the name, address, and telephone number of a person associated with each organization who is familiar with your involvement.

The following two fictional examples will provide an idea on how to formulate the answer to the exemplary conduct request (see chapter 9) found in some pardon applications. Depending on the situation, an applicant's answer may be very different from the examples here. Use the examples only as a guide.

EXEMPLARY CONDUCT EXAMPLES

Example One

John Doe

I take full responsibility for the past crimes in my life. After making some mistakes that I regret, I am now a productive member of society. I have proven my productivity and given back to society in the following ways:

I have lived crime free for the past eight years during which I received my GED. I am now attending General Community College with a GPA of 4.00. I've been on the dean's list for the past two years. My goal is to earn a degree in business management.

At General Community College I developed a support group for adult students who are formerly incarcerated. In the support group, members help other members with stress, coping with life on the outside, tutoring, studying techniques, and homework help.

For the past five years I've volunteered at ABC's Mission to the Homeless where I do light maintenance and landscaping work around the facility. I also maintain the inside of the building by sweeping floors, cleaning dinner tables, washing dishes, and occasionally serving and preparing lunch and dinner meals. At the ABC's Mission I'm in a training program that will allow me to teach adults how to read and write. Feel free to contact my volunteer supervisor Director G. M. Jones at 330-123-4567. I also volunteer (every other weekend) at the local youth detention center where I lecture to young people on the consequences of making the wrong decisions in life.

I received the "Outstanding Volunteer of the Year Award" by the mayor in the city where I reside. A copy of that award is enclosed in the application along with a letter of recognition from the mayor.

I currently work for a roofing company. I would like to one day open my own roofing business (this is where my degree in business management comes in). My goal is to hire other formerly incarcerated individuals, teach them the roofing business, and give ex-inmates the chance I did not initially have. My roofing supervisor, Mr. Wilson, has included a letter of recommendation and his contact information. He is eager to talk with pardon representatives concerning my outstanding work and behavior. I've also included eight letters of support from past employers, professors, counselors, and friends.

Example Two

Betty Doe

When I was incarcerated, I worked very hard to live an exemplary life. I was determined to educate myself and take any and all workshops to further my knowledge and skills. Enclosed in the pardon application you will find a copy of ten certificates of completion from the many workshops I attended while incarcerated. From anger management classes, to counseling, to workshops on parenting, the certificates are intended to prove my determination to become a righteous person for the betterment of my community.

When I was incarcerated, I noticed that many women didn't know how to read or write. I developed a tutoring program and taught 100 fellow inmates reading and writing skills. All 100 women, under my tutoring instruction, pass their GED tests. Once released, my goal was to forever help women who were troubled and in need of assistance. One goal was met with my participation in the "Adult Literacy Now and Today" program in which I tutor adult women in reading and writing skills once a week. You may contact my advisor, Mrs. Jones, at 330-123-4567.

Every year since my release I have participated on a committee that walks many miles for Breast Cancer Awareness. One year, my team raised $1000 for the breast cancer organization. For the past five years since my release, I have also volunteered as a crisis line worker at the SOS Crisis Women's Shelter. While volunteering at the shelter during the day, I take classes at night at the City University where I'm working on my associate's degree. I also hope to work with battered women, or women recovering from addiction. Once a month, I mentor young girls in a program that strives to give young women empowerment and positive role models. The youth program titled "The Strength in Me" encourages girls to stay in school, avoid teenage pregnancy, go to college, and avoid drugs and alcohol.

CHAPTER 7

QUESTIONS ON A PARDON APPLICATION

The questions on a pardon application vary from state to state. The most important thing to remember is to follow the instructions completely and answer each question or section thoroughly.

To get an idea of what may appear on an actual application, the following 13 sections are based on the questions found in the Ohio Parole Board's Application for Executive Clemency.

1-4. Contact Information: The contact information is divided into confined or not confined. If confined (incarcerated), the institution name, number, and the date admitted is required. Also required is the parole eligibility date, post release control date, or end of sentence date. If an individual is not confined and paroled, or released to post release control or community control, a certificate of release is required. In addition, there is a place for a name, an alias, address, city, state, zip, telephone number, age, and date of birth.

5. Type of Clemency Requested: Select pardon, commutation or reprieve.

6. Past Clemency Request: Include the month and year of a denied clemency.

7. Offenses to be Pardoned: List the county, case number, type of crime, date convicted, and the sentence received.

8. Arrest Record: List the county, case number, type of crime, date convicted, and the sentence received.

9. Marital Status: Include the spouse's name and the number of dependents.

10. Job History: List employer's name, address, phone number, and provide the job title.

11. Volunteer Work: Describe any community service or volunteer experience.

12. Reason for Clemency: Explain why clemency is desired. Also, describe any hardship experienced due to the conviction.

13. Additional Information and Attachments: Include letters of recommendation or support (letters from professional people, for instance) and other important documents to aid in pardon consideration including certificates and diplomas.

NOTARY

The Ohio applications must be signed and notarized.

OHIO PARDON APPLICATION REVIEW PROCESS

After all the necessary documents are received by the Ohio Parole Board, a thorough investigation begins. Ohio Revised Code 2967.07.

1. The Ohio Parole Board will initiate an offender background investigation which may involve the following:

   - Interviewing the applicant
   - A questionnaire taken by the applicant

2. An opinion is obtained from the sentencing judge, prosecuting attorney, and arresting agency connected to the applicant's case.

3. Once all opinions are received the completed application is forwarded to the Ohio Parole Board for review.

4. If the application is worthy of consideration the Ohio Parole Board will vote (by majority) to conduct a pardon hearing.

5. After the hearing, the Ohio Parole Board will vote (by majority) to forward a favorable or unfavorable recommendation for pardon to the governor. The governor will make the final decision.

Remember, pardon applications vary from state to state. Use the Ohio application example only as a guide.

OTHER STATE PARDON QUESTIONS

Questions, on other state pardon applications, can range from being asked about naturalized citizenship, to listing the type discharge received from the military (honorable, dishonorable, or bad conduct). In the Vermont pardon application, one must describe "How a pardon will benefit society?" According to the Vermont Governor's Guidelines for Pardon Consideration, the governor wants to see how the pardon will benefit society (not the applicant) in some way. The Illinois pardon application includes a section called "Personal Life History" where a biography is required. The biography may include the description of the rehabilitation programs completed, degrees earned, awards and license received, and other achievements. The Arkansas pardon application asks detailed questions about the victim such as the age of the victim. The Arkansas application also asks if the victim received injuries and if there were more than one victim.

CHAPTER 8

STATE PARDONS GRANTED VERSUS STATE PARDONS DENIED

The following chapter will uncover a glimpse into the contents of actual state pardon applications granted versus actual state pardon applications denied. Federal application examples could not be obtained for this resource. A letter from the pardon attorney revealed the following:

> If you desire access to any applications, we will require the written authorization of the two persons whose applications you desire to review prior to releasing that information to you. The names of individuals whose pardon applications have been granted are listed at our website at, www.justice.gov/pardon, should you require such information.

In addition, I could not acquire what the president based his decision on to grant a particular pardon. The president's decision, I discovered, is confidential. The pardon attorney's Web site explained the restriction:

> The President's decision to grant or deny a petition are generally not disclosed by either the White House or the Department of Justice. In addition, documents reflecting deliberative communications pertaining to presidential decision-making, such as the Department's

recommendation to the President in a clemency matter, are confidential and not available under the Freedom of Information Act.

Source: Number 12, Exclusive Presidential authority. www.usdoj.gov/pardon/pardon_instructions.htm

WHY INCLUDE THIS CHAPTER?

The purpose of this chapter is not to stigmatize those who commit crimes by revealing those crimes in a resource. The chapter may allow comparisons to be made and characteristics of granted and denied applications to be reviewed. The comparisons will hopefully help the reader and potential applicant avoid mistakes and gain insight into traits of favorable pardon applications. The actual names of the applicants, therefore, have been replaced with fictitious names and exact dates are not used. The crimes, sentences, and contents of the applications are factual.

Not every aspect of a state pardon application is public record. Also, not all details of the individual's application are provided in this resource (this also varies from state to state). Some descriptions and application contents may seem sparse.

Enough information is revealed, hopefully, to provide an analysis. Take note of the pardon board recommendations and governors' criteria for a pardon. Also, notice that just because an individual is granted a pardon "hearing" does not mean that same individual will be granted a pardon. In addition, pay close attention to how the applicants turned their lives around (evidence of exemplary conduct which is very important to pardon officials). Remember, pardon officials also take into consideration the victim's opinion pertaining to the pardon, and the witnesses present at the pardon hearing on behalf of (or against) the applicant. For an example of a pardon procedure and review process for the state of Washington see appendix D.

PARDONS DENIED

Fred J. Jonesmith of Tennessee (Caucasian Male)

In 1978, Fred J. Jonesmith, convicted of possession of a controlled substance for resale, served 30 days in the Montgomery County Penal Farm and received three years probation. Fred applied for a pardon for the drug conviction in the year 2000 on the basis of continuing his teaching and furthering his education to the master's degree level. Fred revealed many accomplishments in his application including receiving an honorable discharge from the U.S. Army, earning a bachelor of science degree, and acquiring a teaching certificate. Fred also included many letters of recommendation and commendation which described his outstanding character and included accolades and praise.

Forwarded to the Tennessee Board of Probation and Parole for review, the information in Fred's application seemed to reflect a strong need for a pardon.

Fred received a letter from the board saying that he needed documentation from an "official" source stating that his conviction prevented him from achieving his educational goal. An official source from the master's degree program, for instance.

In the end, the board did not grant Fred a pardon hearing because the governor's criteria for a pardon were not met. According to the board, the governor's criteria states, "Petitioner has demonstrated with proper verification, a specific and compelling need for a pardon." Fred's case did not exemplify a specific and compelling need. In other words, he did not show that his conviction would have deterred his educational pursuits or deny an achievement.

The "proper verification" represented the letter from an official of the master's degree program denying Fred entry into the program. The board requested the denial letter, but Fred did not provide the letter. The lack of verification may have been the deciding factor in Fred's case.

It is very important to follow every instruction requested by the board.

Faith O'Neil of Wisconsin (African American Female)

In 1991, Faith O'Neil, convicted of welfare fraud, received eight years probation and paid restitution (repayment of funds). For four years, O'Neil worked and also received public assistance from the state of Wisconsin.

Faith applied for a pardon to help her achieve the dream of going to nursing school and receiving a nursing license. Faith received discouraging news from the school of her choice. The university official informed her that without a pardon, going to nursing school would be a difficult task. The official said that the Nursing Board may not comment on some convictions (such as Faith's) until license examination time. In other words, Faith could be in school for many years only to realize that she would not be able to take the nursing license test. Also, in order to do clinical work, hospitals would have to give the student permission to work with clients. If the student is denied clinical work, the student will not be able to complete the degree.

Enclosed as part of the pardon application, Faith included certificates of completion for job readiness training, medical billing and coding, and a financial management workshop. Faith also included a transcript from a training center for the medical billing and coding training.

Faith did not receive a pardon. The Wisconsin Pardon Advisory Board acknowledged Faith's positive lifestyle and nonviolent crime but considered the "criminal justice system contacts" in the application.

Alison F. Johnston of Tennessee (Caucasian Female)

In 1993, Alison F. Johnston, convicted of voluntary manslaughter, suffered from physical and emotional abuse at the hands of her boyfriend. Alison had the boyfriend under a court issued Order of Protection before shooting and killing him in self defense. Johnston completed a three year sentence at the Tennessee State Penitentiary for the crime.

After Alison served her sentence, she lived an exemplary life by continuing her nursing education, participating in local health fairs, volunteering with the battered women's organization, and remarrying. Alison applied for a pardon in 2000 based on the belief that she would not be admitted to the nursing program and would not obtain her nursing license.

Forwarded to the Tennessee Board of Pardon and Paroles for review, Alison's application received a pardon recommendation hearing. In Alison's case, three board members recommended a pardon, three board members recommended against a pardon, and one board member withdrew from voting.

The three board members who recommended Governor Sundquit grant Alison a pardon continued (rescheduled) her case, until Alison obtain an official letter from the university stating that her felony prevented her from obtaining a nursing education and license. The board also suggested that Alison apply to the nursing school of her choosing and if she is denied entry, such denial letter is to be forwarded to the board. In Alison's "Notice of Board Action," the board expressed that Alison did not "show a compelling need for pardon." The board also noted to "hold vote" until an official denial letter from the nursing school transpired.

Alison wrote to the board explaining that she could not obtain the necessary documentation of an official denial letter because (she heard) the college would not state such denial publicly. In addition, family members of the victim (Alison's boyfriend) were in attendance at Alison's pardon hearing, which may have also influenced the pardon decision outcome.

Governor Sundquist denied Alison's request for pardon.

Bill Greentree of Maine (Caucasian Male)

In 1992, Bill Greentree, convicted of unlawfully furnishing scheduled drugs, received five years suspended sentence except for six months. Bill also received four years probation and paid a $1,100 fine.

Bill applied for a pardon in 2009 on the basis of being sorry for the crime and turning his life around. Bill failed to understand a very important section of the application that read, "Please describe the 'EXCEPTIONAL circumstances,' that you think would justify the board's consideration of your petition for executive clemency." Bill had an opportunity to prove himself and reveal to the board that he is worthy of a pardon. Instead of submitting proof of accomplishment after accomplishment, Bill enclosed a half page paper describing that he works full time, has positive commitments, wants to go traveling, wants to put the conviction behind him, and is active in church. Greentree did not provide any indication that his conviction threatened a future achievement. There is no evidence or documentation of a denial of a job or denial of a license because of the conviction.

Bill did not receive a pardon hearing.

A letter to Bill from the Governor's Board of Executive Clemency read, "The Board did not find your petition to demonstrate exceptional circumstances to warrant a hearing at this time."

Frederick S. Stanton of New Hampshire (Caucasian Male)

In 2004, Frederick S. Stanton pleaded guilty to three felony charges: accomplice to burglary, accomplice/principle to burglary, and conspiracy to commit burglary. Frederick, with help from two accomplices, broke into an eatery after hours in a three day period and took over $1000 from the business. Stanton received a 2-4 year suspended sentence, two years probation, restitution of $2871.00, drug treatment, counseling, and education programs as part of the conditions of his sentence.

Frederick applied for a pardon in 2008 because he wanted to enlist in the United States Army. According to the Army, however, a pardon would not guarantee his enlistment. The Army denied Stanton a moral waiver on the grounds that his crimes fell under the classification of Serious Criminal Misconduct (Army Regulation 601-210, 4-11, f). The Army considered Frederick's crimes "non-waiverable" (AR 601-210, 4-24, p). The Army recruiter informed Mr. Stanton of this fact.

Also, a poor review came from the county attorney. The attorney did not recommend a pardon for Frederick because of the seriousness of the crimes and the feelings of the victim who, although believed in forgiveness, did not think enough time had passed for Frederick to make a positive difference in his life.

Frederick's pardon application included information concerning several parole violations (in one violation he failed a drug test), but Frederick completed an in-patient substance abuse treatment program.

About 15 letters of support expressing how Stanton had changed his life for the better by overcoming his addictions, including letters of recommendation from the treatment facility that helped (and now employ) Stanton, made up the pardon application.

The conclusion to this story: Frederick did not receive a pardon. The two primary factors that may have influenced the pardon denial are the victim's statement against the pardon and the county attorney's unfavorable recommendation.

PARDONS GRANTED

Stella Morningview of Maine (Caucasian Female)

In 1995, Stella Morningview, convicted of assault, received five days suspended sentence with one year probation. After the conviction, Stella committed no other crime. In 2008, Stella applied for a pardon for the assault based on the possibility of losing her job at the gun manufacturing company where she worked.

In Stella's case, the BATF (Bureau of Alcohol, Tobacco, Firearms and Explosives) jeopardized the jobs of employees at the gun company who were not supposed to possess firearms. Stella never worried about applying for a pardon (for her 13 year old conviction) before this situation. The BATF's actions, however, threatened a career spanning 20 years. For Stella, the loss of a job would have created a hardship.

Threatened with the loss of a job after 20 years of employment (as well as living a crime free life), must have satisfied the governor's criteria of "exceptional circumstances." The governor granted Stella a pardon.

To review the actual pardon certificate see appendix E.

Summer Jamison of Wisconsin (African American Female)

In 1996, Summer Jamison, charged with food stamp and Aid to Dependent Children fraud, received five years probation. Summer also paid back the entire fraud amount of over $20,000. Summer, expected to report her income, would report income sometimes and other times she would not report income. After the conviction, Summer committed no other crimes.

In 2009, Summer applied for a pardon because she wanted to reach her "highest potential." Summer proved over and over her determination to reach "high potential." For instance, after receiving an associate in applied science, and a bachelor of science degree, she began working on a master's degree.

According to Summer, the crime made her a stronger and better person because she realized the opportunities lost and the "potentials" she once had before the conviction. The barriers that slowed Summer's path made her work even harder to achieve her goals. Not only did Summer express she wanted to represent something to the community, but she wanted to give back to the community as well. Summer seemed so confident in her summary of "Explanation of why Clemency is needed," that her primary educational achievement included the goal to one day become an attorney.

Summer provided nine letters of support and recommendation from various sources such as university officials, employers, and others. Summer also included college and university transcripts and related diplomas. Seven certificates of completion were also enclosed in the application from educational and training workshops.

In 2010, the governor of Wisconsin granted Summer a pardon because of her "hard-work and transition into a productive, law-abiding member of the community."

Theodore Ramone of Tennessee (Caucasian Male)

In 1987, Theodore Ramone delivered and sold 30 grams of cocaine for $10,000 to an undercover narcotics agent. In 1988, Theodore pleaded guilty and served eighteen months of a seven year sentence. After his discharge from parole of four years, Ramone committed no other crime.

Theodore applied for a pardon in 1999 based on his belief that his felony conviction would prevent his admission to the state and federal bar and jeopardize future employment as an attorney.

Theodore lived an exemplary life after completing his sentence. For instance, Theodore received a bachelor of science, a master of science, an artium magister degree, and published scholarly works.

Ramone received a pardon hearing; however, the hearing continued (rescheduled) until Ramone could provide the Tennessee Board of Probation and Parole evidence of his felony preventing admission to the bar and deterring law related employment opportunities. A legal job offer came to Theodore from Indiana. Theodore presented the necessary evidence to the board in the form of the Admission and Discipline Rule 12 of the Indiana Rules of Court. The rule explains the general qualifications to be admitted to practice law in Indiana. A portion of Rule 12, Section 2 reads, "Anyone who has been convicted of a felony prima facie shall be deemed lacking the requisite of good moral character as defined in this section."

The evidence of Admission and Discipline Rule 12 of the Indiana Rules of Court, and other evidence of positive lifestyle factors (including educational achievements) in Theodore's application must have fulfilled Governor Sundquist's requirement of a specific and compelling need for pardon.

Governor Sundquist granted Theodore a pardon.

Sebastain Ferdinand of Wisconsin (African-American Male)

In 1993, Sebastain Ferdinand, charged with delivery of controlled substance and possession with intent to deliver controlled substance, served two years in prison. In 1995, charged with the same offense, possession with intent to deliver controlled substance, Ferdinand served eight years in prison.

In 2008, Sebastian applied for a pardon on the basis of furthering his career within the Department of Defense because some jobs in the department required a higher security clearance.

In Sebastain's narrative of why he is requesting a pardon, he expressed responsibility for his crimes, acceptance of his punishment, admitted his wrong doing, and asked the Wisconsin Pardon Advisory Board for forgiveness. Sebastain conveyed remorse for the crimes and emphasized his desire to do all that he can, "whatever I can," to right the wrongs of the past. In his quest to do the right thing, Sebastain got married, joined a church, went back to school (technical college), and rejoined the U.S. Army Reserve where he served for six years.

Sebastain's desire to prove his worthiness for a pardon is seen in his loyalty to his country when he did not hesitate to serve over in Iraq for the military. As a result of his military service, Sebastain received the Army Achievement Medal, the Commander's Certificate of Excellence, an Army Training Certificate of Completion, and three Army Certificates of Appreciation.

In 2010, the governor of Wisconsin granted Sebastain a pardon.

Phillip Peterman of New Hampshire (Caucasian Male)

In 2000, Phillip Peterman, charged with two misdemeanor simple assault convictions, received 60 days suspended sentence for one year on the condition that he commit no other crime, attend anger management classes, and go to AA meetings once a week.

Phillip applied for a pardon in 2003 on the basis that his convictions jeopardized his deployment overseas to Iraq with his unit in the military. Under the Lautenberg Amendment to the Gun Control Act of 1968, Phillip could not possess a firearm.

WHAT IS THE LAUTENBERG AMENDMENT?

According to the Lautenberg Amendment to the Gun Control Act of 1968, enacted in 1996, it is a felony to possess, transport, ship or receive firearms or ammunition for individuals convicted of misdemeanor crimes of domestic violence. Title 18 USC § (g)(9).

Phillip's application included several letters of support, and a letter from the director of the agency confirming his completion of anger management classes. The application also included a letter from his captain from the Army National Guard, the presiding judge in Phillip's case, two letters from friends of Phillip, and letters in support from the victims in the case. The victims in the case included Phillip's wife and son. Phillip's wife and son also provided positive testimony on behalf of Phillip at the pardon hearing.

By unanimous vote, the governor and the Executive Council granted Phillip a pardon.

CHAPTER 9

STATE-BY-STATE PARDON CONTACT AND ELIGIBILITY INFORMATION

**(Including the evidence of exemplary conduct request
found in almost all state pardon applications)**

ALABAMA

Executive Clemency
Alabama Constitution Article V, Section 124

> It is the responsibility of the Alabama Pardon Unit
> (Board) to investigate and process pardons, voter rights
> restoration, and remissions of find and forfeiture. What
> is remission of fines and forfeitures?

Remission of Fines and Forfeitures
Remission of fine means one does not have to pay back a fine. Remission
of forfeiture means the giving back of a person's property (and rights to
property) that was taken away because of the conviction.

Pardon Eligibility
The sentence must be completed, or three years completion of permanent
parole. Alabama Code § 15-22-36(c).

Pardon Contact Information
To receive a pardon application contact the Alabama Board of
Pardons:

Alabama Board of Pardons and Paroles
301 South Ripley Street
P.O. Box 302405
Montgomery, Alabama 36130-2405
334-353-7771
Fax: 334-242-1809
http://paroles.state.al.us

Additional Information
According to the Alabama Pardon Unit of the Board of Pardons and
Paroles, when requesting a pardon in writing the applicant must do the
following:

1. Indicate that he or she is requesting a pardon for a misdemeanor
   or felony.
2. Include his or her name and contact information.

3. List the convictions and provide the year and county of the convictions.
4. Provide a work phone number.
5. Include an Alabama prison number (if applicable).
6. Identify the conviction as state or federal.
7. Include Social Security number, date of birth, sex and race.

**See Pardon Board Web site for the complete list.

Note: In 1939, an amendment to the Alabama Constitution gave pardon power to the legislature which passed pardon authority to the Alabama Board of Pardons.

ALASKA

Executive Clemency
Alaska Constitution Article III, Section 21

> Only the governor has the authority to grant pardons, reprieves, and commute a sentence. The governor also grants amnesty and remits fines and forfeiture. What is amnesty?

Amnesty
Amnesty is provided for the restoration of peace after political unrest. It is a kind of pardon that is given to a group of people for the same offense.

Eligibility
The informational booklet Executive Clemency in Alaska states that after the applicant has completed his or her sentence "a significant period of time" has to pass before a pardon will be granted. The applicant must also reveal "complete and total rehabilitation."

Contact Information
Before an individual can receive an application for pardon in Alaska, a Clemency Eligibility Determination Form must be filled out and returned to the Alaska Board of Parole.

To request a Clemency Eligibility Determination Form contact the Alaska Board of Parole:

Alaska Board of Parole
Attn: Clemency Determination
550 West 7th Avenue, Suite 601
Anchorage, Alaska 99501
907-770-6310
Fax: 907-770-6308
Forms may also be obtained from the Web site:
http://www.correct.state.ak.us/corrections/Parole/paroleboard.jsf

Evidence of Exemplary Conduct

In the Alaska Board of Parole Clemency Worksheet (application), at the section titled "Statement," the applicant may use the whole page and additional pages to include achievements and accomplishments to enhance his or her pardon worthiness. The worksheet requests that the applicant state the reasons for clemency:

> Petitioner respectfully requests that he/she be granted clemency for the following reasons (provide a statement or a list of all factors which you believe should be considered in your favor; use an extra sheet of paper if necessary).

ARIZONA

Executive Clemency
Arizona Constitution Article V, Section 5

> The governor grants pardons, commutations, and reprieves after recommendation from the Arizona Board of Executive Clemency.

Eligibility
A person may apply for a pardon after the completion of a prison term (Love, 2007).

Contact Information
To receive a pardon application contact the Arizona Board of Executive Clemency:

Arizona Board of Executive Clemency
1645 West Jefferson, Suite 101
Phoenix, Arizona 85007
602-542-5656
Fax: 602-542-5680
www.azboec.gov

Additional Information
According to Arizona Revised Statutes § 13-910, a felony conviction suspends certain rights such as the following:

- The right to serve on a jury.
- The right to vote.
- The right to hold public office.

1. When an individual applies for a pardon the Arizona Board of Executive Clemency will ask the judge and county attorney related to the case to provide the facts of the individual's trial. Arizona Revised Statues § 31-441.
2. Once released from prison, or once probation is completed and restitution is paid, a first felony offender's civil rights are automatically restored. Arizona Revised Statues § 13-912.

3. Once released from federal prison, an individual may, two years after date of total discharge, apply for restoration of civil rights. Arizona Revised Statues § 13-910.

Arkansas

Executive Clemency
Arkansas Constitution Article VI, Section 18

> The governor has the power to grant executive clemency in the form of pardons, commutation of sentence, the forgiveness of fines or forfeiture, and reprieves. The governor grants pardons after recommendation from the Arkansas Parole Board.

Eligibility
No requirements. Source: Parole Services.

Contact Information
To receive a pardon application contact the Arkansas Parole Board:

Arkansas Parole Board
Two Union National Plaza Building
105 West Capitol Avenue, Suite 500
Little Rock, Arkansas 72201
501-682-3850
To download an application visit:
http://paroleboard.arkansas.gov

Additional Information
According to the Arkansas Parole Board Annual Report 2007-08, "A pardon request asks that a criminal record be expunged or removed from the public record."

Evidence of Exemplary Conduct
In the Arkansas pardon application, the request for evidence of exemplary conduct emphasizes rehabilitation:

> Describe what you have done to demonstrate your rehabilitation—community programs, volunteer work, furthering education, speaking engagements, mentoring to others, etc.

CALIFORNIA

Executive Clemency
California Constitution Article V, Section 8

> The governor has the power to grant reprieves, pardons, and commutations.

Eligibility
In How to Apply for a Pardon from the office of the governor, a 10 year wait is required after probation or parole.

Contact Information
To receive a pardon application contact the governor's office:

Governor's Office
State Capital
Attention: Legal Affairs Secretary
Sacramento, California 95814
916-445-281
http://www.gov.ca.gov

Additional Information
To start the pardon process an individual first applies for a Certificate of Rehabilitation. The certificate is an indication that the person is rehabilitated. Once the certificate is granted, the certificate turns into the application for pardon which will be forwarded to the governor. For more information on the Certificate of Rehabilitation see Penal Code 4852.01 to 4852.21.

People who are not eligible for a Certificate of Rehabilitation may apply for a traditional pardon. For more information about the traditional pardon consult Penal Code sections 4800-4813.

Evidence of Exemplary Conduct
Under the section of the pardon application titled Pardon Based on Rehabilitation, the request for evidence of exemplary conduct says, "Describe your rehabilitation and activities since release."

COLORADO

Executive Clemency
Colorado Constitution Article IV, Section 7

> Executive clemency in Colorado is in the form of a pardon and commutation of sentence. The governor has authority to grant clemency after recommendation from the Colorado Executive Clemency Advisory Board.

Eligibility
A 10 year wait is required after sentence is completed. Source: governor's office applicant instructions.

Contact Information
To receive a pardon application contact the following:

Clemency Director
Colorado Department of Corrections
8800 Sheridan Boulevard
Westminster Colorado 80031-3405
303-426-6198
Fax: 303-426-1354
www.doc.state.co.us

Additional Information
The governor's office applicant instructions state the following:

1. The Colorado Executive Clemency Advisory Board has the responsibility to review pardon applications.

2. The governor has the final decision concerning the pardon.

3. The pardon does not seal or expunge the criminal record.

Evidence of Exemplary Conduct
The request for evidence of exemplary conduct says, "List any awards, hobbies, clubs, organizations, charities or other similar organizations you belong to."

CONNECTICUT

Executive Clemency
Connecticut General Statutes, Chapter 961, Section 54-124a

> The Connecticut Board of Pardons and Paroles has the sole power to issue pardons. The governor grants reprieves. Connecticut Constitution Article 4 § 13.

Eligibility
In the Connecticut pardon procedures, an individual must wait five years after the conviction for a felony to apply for a pardon.

Contact Information
To receive a pardon application contact the Connecticut Board of Pardons:

State of Connecticut
Board of Pardons & Paroles
55 West Main Street
Waterbury, Connecticut 06702
(800) 303-2884
203-805-6605
Fax: 203-805-6630
An application may also be obtained from the Web site:
http://www.ct.gov/doc/bopp

Additional Information
If a pardon is granted, state attorney's files and court and police records connected to the conviction are erased (expunged). Connecticut General Statutes § 54-142 a(d).

Evidence of Exemplary Conduct
In the Connecticut Application for an Expungement or Provisional Pardon, the volunteer section says, "Describe any charitable, volunteer, church or civic activities in which you have been engaged or other contributions you have made to the community since your conviction."

DELAWARE

Executive Clemency
Delaware Constitution Article VII, Section 1

> The governor grants pardons in Delaware after recommendation from the Delaware Board of Pardons. The governor does not have to accept the board's recommendation. The governor may also remit fines and forfeiture, commute a sentence, and grant reprieves.

Eligibility
According to the Delaware secretary of state, a five year wait is required after sentence is completed.

Contact Information
To receive a pardon application contact the Delaware secretary of state:

Secretary of State's Office
401 Federal Street, Suite 3
Dover, Delaware 19901
302-739-4111
Fax: 302-739-7654
Information on how to prepare an application packet can be found at the Web site:
http://pardons.delaware.gov

Additional Information
In Delaware, the pardon application is prepared by the applicant. There is no standard form. It is up to the applicant, therefore, to gather the necessary documents and detailed data and file the application with the appropriate office.

Evidence of Exemplary Conduct
According to the Delaware Board of Pardon's Instructions for Filing a Petition for Pardon, the fourth step in the application process says, "On a separate sheet of paper, please state your Reasons for Applying and why you believe you should be considered for a pardon."

DISTRICT OF COLUMBIA

Executive Clemency
Violations of the city code ordinances are pardoned by the mayor of the District of Columbia:

> The Mayor of the District of Columbia may grant pardons and respites for offenses against the late corporation of Washington, the ordinances of Georgetown and the levy court, the laws enacted by the Legislative Assembly, and the police and building regulations of the District. D.C. ST § 1-301.76.

Violations of the D.C. Code are pardoned by the president of the United States. An application may be obtained from the office of the pardon attorney.

Eligibility
Applicants must wait five years after the date of release from incarceration or conviction for a presidential pardon (28 Code of Federal Regulations § 1.2). Contact the mayor of the District of Columbia for city code violation pardon eligibility.

Contact Information
To begin the executive clemency process by pardon for violations of the D.C. Code contact the pardon attorney:

Office of the Pardon Attorney
U.S. Department of Justice
1425 New York Avenue N.W.
Washington, DC 20530-0001
202.616.6070

Pardon applications and information about the presidential pardon procedure may also be acquired from the pardon attorney's Web site: www.usdoj.gov/pardon

For information on mayoral pardons write to the mayor:

Executive Office of the Mayor
1350 Pennsylvania Avenue, NW, Suite 316
Washington, D.C. 20004
www.dc.gov/mayor/index.shtm

FLORIDA

Executive Clemency
Florida Constitution Article IV, Section 8(a)

> In Florida, the governor, with agreement from two clemency board members, has the power to grant clemency. Executive clemency in Florida consists of full pardon, restoration of civil rights, remission of fine and forfeiture, and the granting of reprieves.

Eligibility
A person may apply for a pardon 10 years after completion of a sentence. Source: Rule 5 of Florida Rules of Executive Clemency.

Contact Information
To receive a pardon application contact the Office of Executive Clemency:

Coordinator
Office of Executive Clemency
2601 Blair Stone Road
Building C, Room 229
Tallahassee, Florida 32399-2450
850-488-2952
Applications may also be obtained from the Web site:
https://fpc.state.fl.us/Clemency.htm

Additional Information
According to the Florida Information and Instructions on Applying for Clemency, the Executive Clemency Board will look at the following characteristics when considering a pardon:

- Work history of the applicant
- Letters for or against the pardon
- Additional arrests or traffic violations
- Outstanding debts including child support
- Any history of addiction or mental disability

GEORGIA

Executive Clemency
Georgia Constitution Article IV, Section 2

> The Georgia Board of Pardons and Paroles has the authority to grant pardons. The board also grants commutations and restoration of civil and political rights.

Eligibility
A pardon seeker must live five years crime free, meet all conditions of his or her sentence, and have no sentence-related fines. Source: Georgia State Board of Pardons and Paroles.

Contact Information
To receive a pardon application contact the Georgia Board of Pardons and Paroles:

State Board of Pardons and Paroles
2 Martin Luther King Jr., Drive S.E.
Balcony Level, East Tower
Atlanta, Georgia 30334-4909
404-656-5651
Applications may also be obtained from the Web site:
www.pap.state.ga.us

Additional Information
An individual with a felony involving moral turpitude loses certain rights such as the right to serve on a jury, hold public office, and the right to vote. To restore lost rights, an individual may apply for restoration of civil and political rights under Georgia law. The right to vote is restore automatically after the completion of the sentence.

Evidence of Exemplary Conduct
In the Georgia pardon application, the request for evidence of good conduct says, "List all honors, awards or achievements which you have accomplished since your conviction."

HAWAII

Executive Clemency
Hawaii Constitution Article V, Section 5

> Pardons are granted by the governor after recommendation from the Hawaii Paroling Authority. The governor also has the power to grant reprieves and commutations.

Eligibility
In the Hawaii Parole Handbook, all convicted felons are eligible for a pardon once parole or probation requirements are satisfied, and the applicant has proved worthiness through crime free behavior.

Contact Information
To receive a pardon application contact the Hawaii Paroling Authority:

Hawaii Paroling Authority
Attention: Paroles and Pardons Administrator
1177 Alakea Street, Ground Floor
Honolulu, Hawaii 96813
Applications may also be obtained from the Paroling Authority Web site:
http://hawaii.gov/psd/attached-agencies/hpa

A parole officer will conduct an investigation and provide a report and recommendation to the governor within 45 days.

Evidence of Exemplary Conduct
Applicants can provide evidence of exemplary conduct by listing achievements at part 12 and 13 on the Hawaii pardon application which says, "I belong to the following organizations and activities (including church affiliation)." In addition, the application reads, "The reasons I am asking for a pardon are."

Idaho

Executive Clemency
Idaho Constitution Article IV, Section 7

> The Idaho Commission of Pardons and Parole has the sole power to grant pardons. The commission also grants commutations and the remission of fines and forfeiture.

Eligibility
In Idaho, a pardon seeker with a nonviolent crime must wait three years after completing a sentence before applying for a pardon. Idaho Administrative Code Rules of the Commission of Pardons and Parole IDAPA 50.01.01 § 550(a).

For individuals with sex crimes or violent convictions, a five year wait is required. IDAPA 50.01.01 § 550(b).

Contact Information
To receive a pardon application contact the Idaho Commission of Pardons and Parole:

State of Idaho Commission of Pardons and Parole
PO Box 83720
Statehouse Mail
Boise, Idaho 83720-1807
208-334-2520
Applications may also be obtained from the Web site:
http://www2.state.id.us/parole

Additional Information
According to the Idaho Administrative Code Rules of the Commission of Pardons and Parole (IDAPA 50-01-01, § 550-2 (b)), when reviewing pardon applications the board will investigate the following characteristics of the applicant:

- Employment history
- Criminal record
- Status as a good individual

Evidence of Exemplary Conduct

The Idaho pardon application says, "State reasons you feel a pardon is needed."

ILLINOIS

Executive Clemency
Illinois Constitution Article V, Section 12

> Executive clemency in Illinois is in the form of commutation of sentence, reprieve, and pardon. The governor has final authority to grant clemency including pardons.

Eligibility
No restrictions. An individual may apply any time (Love, 2007).

Contact Information
In Illinois, it is the Prisoner Review Board's job to analyze applications for pardon and forward recommendations to the governor. Chapter 730 Illinois Compiled Statutes 5/3-3-2.

To receive a pardon application contact the Illinois Prisoner Review Board:

Illinois Prisoner Review Board
319 East Madison, Suite A
Springfield, Illinois 62701
217-782-7273
Applications may also be obtained from the Web site:
www.state.il.us/prb

Evidence of Exemplary Conduct
The Illinois pardon application requests evidence of exemplary conduct in the "Personal Life History" section:

> You may also include information or degrees or diplomas earned or anticipated, awards of commendations at school or work, counseling or rehabilitation programs you have attended or completed, military awards, civil or occupational licenses or certifications, and life changing events.

INDIANA

Executive Clemency
Indiana Constitution Article V, Section 17

> In Indiana the governor has the power to grant executive clemency in the form of commutation of sentence, pardon, and reprieve.

Eligibility
According to the Indiana Parole Board, an individual must wait five years after the completion of the sentence before a pardon application consideration.

Contact Information
To receive a pardon application contact the Indiana Parole Board:

Indiana Parole Board
302 West Washington Street, Room E321
Indianapolis, Indiana 46204-2278
317-232-5737
Fax: 317-232-5738
Applications may also be obtained from the Web site:
www.in.gov/idoc/2324.htm

Evidence of Exemplary Conduct
In the Indiana Pardon Application, there is one whole page devoted to evidence of exemplary conduct titled "The Following Information will be needed in Completing Your Pardon Application." The page encourages the applicant to reveal good conduct and to list examples including the following: medals received, positive activities accomplished, skills from employment, degrees earned, and the letters of recommendation from friends and family.

At the bottom of the exemplary conduct page the applicant is assured that the information provided is helpful for pardon consideration. The supplement says, "All of the above will allow you to present the Parole Board with evidence of the positive activities you have been involved in since your offense."

IOWA

Executive Clemency
Iowa Constitution IV, Section 16

> According to the Iowa Constitution, the governor has the power to grant executive clemency which comes in the forms of pardon, commutation of sentence, and reprieves.

The application instructions, from the office of the governor, considers restoration of citizenship rights (the right to vote and hold public office), and special restoration of citizenship (firearms rights) as part of the governor's clemency power.

Eligibility
The application instructions state that the governor prefers those seeking a pardon to wait at least 10 years from the discharge date of a sentence to submit a pardon application.

Contact Information
To receive a pardon application contact the Iowa General Counsel:

General Counsel
Governor's Office
State Capitol Building
Des Moines, Iowa 50319
515-281-5211
Applications may also be obtained from the Web site:
www.governor.iowa.gov/files/app-clemency.pdf

Evidence of Exemplary Conduct
The evidence of exemplary conduct request in the Iowa pardon application says, "List all honors, awards or achievements which you have accomplished since your conviction."

The application also says, "List all community service or volunteer service projects that you have participated in since your conviction including name, address, and phone numbers of the contact person(s) affiliated with the project."

KANSAS

Executive Clemency
Kansas Constitution Article I, Section 7

> The governor of Kansas has the sole authority to grant pardons. The Kansas Parole Board analyzes the application information and sends recommendations to the governor.

Eligibility
A person may apply at any time. Only state ex-offenders are eligible. Kansas Statutes § 22-3701.

Contact Information
To receive a pardon application contact the Kansas Parole Board:

Kansas Parole Board
Landon State Office Building
900 SW Jackson, Suite 425-S
Topeka, Kansas 66612-1220
785-296-3469

Instructions and an application may be obtained from the Web site:
www.dc.state.ks.us/kpb/clemency

Additional Information
According to the Kansas Parole Board's instructions for clemency, the pardon application materials must include the following:

A. Notice of Clemency Application-Sentencing Form.
One copy of the completed form must be sent within the county of conviction to the following:
- Police Chief
- Judge
- Prosecuting Attorney
- Sheriff

B. Request for Publication Form—applicants must send two copies to the county newspaper.

C. Application for Clemency—applicants must complete two copies of the application.

Evidence of Exemplary Conduct

The evidence of exemplary conduct request says, "Reason for seeking Clemency (use extra page is needed)."

KENTUCKY

Executive Clemency
Kentucky Constitution Section 77 and 150

> The governor grants pardons, commutes sentences, and issues the restoration of civil rights.

Eligibility
A 10 year wait is preferred after sentence is completed. Source: Pardon application instructions.

Contact Information
Pardon applications may be obtained from the governor's office:

Office of the General Counsel
Office of the Governor
700 Capitol Avenue, Room 100
Frankfort, Kentucky 40601
502-564-2611
Fax: 502-564-2517
www.governor.ky.gov

People interested in the restoration of civil rights must request an application from the Department of Corrections:

Kentucky Department of Corrections
Division of Probation and Parole
Attn: Restoration of Civil Rights
PO Box 2400
Frankfort, Kentucky 40602-2400
www.corrections.ky.gov

Evidence of Exemplary Conduct
The evidence of good conduct request in the Kentucky pardon application reads, "In separate letter, which must accompany the application, please describe in your own words the reason(s) you are seeking relief and state the extenuating circumstances supporting the basis for the request."

LOUISIANA

Executive Clemency
Louisiana Constitution Article IV, Section 5(E)(1)

> The governor may grant pardons, reprieves, remit fines and forfeitures, and commute sentences after recommendation from the Louisiana Board of Pardons.

Eligibility
Once a sentence is completed, a nonviolent first offender (first felony offense) is pardoned automatically without assistance from the governor. Louisiana Revised Statutes Ann. §15:572(B) (1). Violent offenders must apply for full pardon.

Contact Information
To receive a pardon application contact the Louisiana Board of Pardons:

Louisiana Board of Pardons
PO Box 94304
Baton Rouge, Louisiana 70804-9304
225-342-5421
Fax: 225-342-2289
An application may also be obtained from the Web site:
www.corrections.state.la.us/files/pardon/APPLICATION.pdf

Additional Information
The Louisiana Board of Pardons Rules
Only the application and necessary attachments must be sent to the board. Other information such as letters of recommendation, employment information, and certificates of achievement may be sent after the applicant is notified of a hearing.

See Rule 2 "Filing Procedure" for information needed for the pardon application.

If the application is denied an individual must wait two years to reapply, according to Rule 3 of the Board of Pardons Rules.

Evidence of Executive Clemency
The Louisiana application simply says, "Reason for requesting Clemency."

MAINE

Executive Clemency
Maine Constitution Article V, Part 1, Section 11

> In Maine, executive clemency is in the form of a pardon and commutation of sentence. The governor of Maine has the authority to grant executive clemency after recommendation from the Governor's Board of Executive Clemency.

Eligibility
A five year wait after sentence is completed is required. Source: Maine secretary of state.

Contact Information
To receive a pardon application contact the Maine secretary of state:

Office of the Secretary of State
Bureau of Corporations, Elections and Commissions
101 State House Station
Augusta, Maine 04333
207-624-7752
An application may also be acquired from the Web site:
www.maine.gov/sos/cec/boards/pardons.htm

Additional Information
In the Maine secretary of state Web site, clemency section, Maine pardon applications will not be considered if the following is evident:

1. The applicant is using the pardon to request his or her name be taken off the sex offender list.
2. The applicant is using the pardon to enter Canada.
3. The applicant's goal is to right the wrongs in the system of justice.
4. The applicant wants to carry a firearm.
5. The applicant wants the pardon for only one conviction when the offender committed several crimes not listed on the pardon application.

Evidence of Exemplary Conduct

The evidence of exemplary conduct request in the Maine application for pardon says, "Please describe the EXCEPTIONAL circumstances that you think would justify the Board's consideration of your petition for executive clemency."

MARYLAND

Executive Clemency
Maryland Constitution Article II, Section 20

> The governor has the power to grant pardons and commute sentences.

Eligibility
According to the Maryland Parole Commission "Frequently Asked Questions," people with felonies must wait 10 years crime free, and people with misdemeanors must wait five years crime free, before being considered for a pardon. People with violent felonies or convicted of a crime concerning controlled dangerous substances must wait 20 years crime free.

Contact Information
To receive a pardon application contact the Maryland Parole Commission:

Maryland Parole Commission
6776 Reisterstown Road, Suite 307
Baltimore, Maryland 21215-2343
410-585-3200
Fax: 410-764-4355
1-877-241-5428 (toll free)
www.dpscs.state.md.us
See "About DPSCS, Frequently Asked Questions,
Maryland Parole Commission."

Additional Information
In the Maryland Parole Commission "Frequently Asked Questions," some factors that will be considered for pardon include the following:

- The evidence of rehabilitation.
- The health and age of the applicant.
- The nature of the crime.

Simone R. Richardson

Evidence of Exemplary Conduct

The section titled Interest and Leisure Activities of the Maryland pardon application says, "Describe any charitable or civic activities in which you have been engaged, or other contributions you have made to the community."

MASSACHUSETTS

Executive Clemency
Massachusetts Constitution Chapter 2, Section 1, Article VIII

> The governor has the sole authority to grant pardons and commutations with advice from the Massachusetts Governor's Council.

Eligibility
In the Massachusetts Executive Clemency Guidelines, the individual must live crime free for 15 years for felony convictions. An individual must live crime free for 10 years for misdemeanor convictions.

Contact Information
To receive a pardon application contact the following:

Executive Clemency Coordinator
Executive Clemency Unit
12 Mercer Road
Natick, Massachusetts 01760
508-650-4542
www.mass.gov

Additional Information
In the Executive Clemency Guidelines, the governor will consider the following in the pardon application:

- Evidence of good citizenship and achievement
- Evidence of a "compelling need"
- Compelling need can include a letter from an employer or employment license holder stating that hiring will not take place unless a pardon is granted
- Letter from three individuals revealing positive qualities about the pardon seeker

Evidence of Exemplary Conduct
The section titled Community Achievements in the Massachusetts pardon application reveals the evidence of exemplary conduct request:

Petitioners must demonstrate a substantial period of good citizenship since conviction. Good citizenship shall mean both incident free behavior (but dispositions which are not exculpatory, such as, continuances without a finding, filings, or no-contest pleas, may not be considered incident free behavior) and specific achievements.

MICHIGAN

Executive Clemency
Michigan Constitution Article 5, Section 14

> The governor has the authority to grant commutation
> of sentence, reprieves, and pardons.

Eligibility
No restriction. An individual may apply at anytime (Love, 2007).

Contact Information
To receive a pardon application contact the Michigan Department of
Corrections:

> Michigan Department of Corrections
> Office of the Parole Board
> Pardon and Commutation Coordinator
> Post Office Box 30003
> Lansing, Michigan 48909
> 517-335-1426
> An application may also be obtained from the Web site:
> www.michigan.gov/corrections

Additional Information
In a letter from the office of the Michigan Parole Board, the board
determines if an application is worthy or has merit and if so the following
will occur:

- The prosecutor and judge in the case will then be asked to
  give their opinion concerning the pardon application.
- A public hearing is held if the prosecutor and judge's
  opinions are favorable.
- The board sends the application and a recommendation
  to the governor's office for a final decision.

Evidence of Exemplary Conduct
In Michigan, there are two types of pardon applications: Application
for Pardon after Parole or Discharge, and Application for Pardon or

Commutation of Sentence (for people currently incarcerated). The Application for Pardon after Parole or Discharge requests evidence of good conduct by simply saying, "Attach a brief statement explaining why you are requesting a pardon."

MINNESOTA

Executive Clemency
Minnesota Constitution Article V, Section 7

> The Minnesota Board of Pardons has the authority to grant reprieves and pardons.

Eligibility
According to the Minnesota Board of Pardons, a five year crime free wait, after the completion of a sentence, is required before individuals can apply for a pardon. A ten year crime free wait, after the completion of a sentence, is required for people convicted of a violent crime.

Contact Information
To receive a pardon application contact the Minnesota Board of Pardons:

> Minnesota Board of Pardons
> 1450 Energy Park Drive Suite 200
> St. Pal Minnesota 55108-5219
> 651-642-0284

Evidence of Exemplary Conduct
The evidence of exemplary conduct request is found in the instruction letter accompanying the pardon application from the secretary to the Board of Pardons:

> The Board is particularly interested in hearing about your involvement in the community and any accomplishments that would warrant their attention, and appreciates having at least one other person appear with you at the hearing who can speak about your growth and accomplishments.

The Minnesota pardon application says, "Explain your current personal situation, including information on family, education, achievements, community involvement, treatment/counseling efforts, etc."

MISSISSIPPI

Executive Clemency
Mississippi Constitution Article V, Section 124

> The governor has sole authority to grant pardons, remit fines and forfeiture, and grant reprieves.

Eligibility
A seven year wait is required after discharge of all supervision. Source: Mississippi Parole Board.

Contact Information

Mississippi Parole Board
201 West Capitol Street, Suite 800
Jackson, Mississippi 39201
601-354-7716
www.mdoc.state.ms.us

Additional Information
1. At the governor's request, the Parole Board has the authority to investigate pardon applications. Mississippi Code. Ann §47-7-5(3).
2. The pardon may restore employment to those working as school teachers. Mississippi Code Ann. § 37-9-17(3).
3. A person with a felony may receive a Certificate of Rehabilitation from the court where the conviction was obtained. Mississippi Code Ann. § 97-37-5(3). The certificate is issued to the individual as an indication of rehabilitation and is the courts satisfaction that the individual has lived a crime free life since the completion of the sentence.

MISSOURI

Executive Clemency
Missouri Constitution Article IV, Section 7

> The power to grant a pardon is the responsibility of the governor. The governor also has the authority to grant reprieves and commutations. The two types of pardons include full or partial pardons.

Full Pardon—relieves the collateral consequences of a conviction.
Partial Pardon—limited restoration of rights.

Eligibility
The Missouri Department of Correction Web site "Eligibility Criteria" section states that a three year wait after sentence is completed, including prison, probation, or parole is required.

Contact Information
To receive a pardon application contact the Missouri Board of Probation and Parole:

Board of Probation and Parole
1511 Christy Drive
Jefferson City, Missouri 65101
573-751-6588
Fax: 573-751-8501

Executive clemency applications may be obtained from the Web site:
http://doc.mo.gov/division/prob/ExecClem.php

Additional Information
According to the Missouri Department of Corrections, collateral consequences of a conviction may include the denial of the right to do the following:

- Vote. Revised Statutes of Missouri 115.133
- Hold public office (until sentence is complete). Revised Statutes of Missouri 561.021

- Serve on a jury. Revised Statutes of Missouri 561.026

Evidence of Exemplary Conduct

The Missouri application requests evidence of exemplary conduct with one line: "What is your reason for making application at this time?"

Montana

Executive Clemency
Montana Constitution Article VI, Section 12

> The authority to grant pardons, commute sentences, remit fines and forfeiture, and restore citizenship rests with the governor.

Eligibility
A person may apply at any time. Montana Code Ann. 46-23-301(2).

Contact Information
To receive a pardon application contact the Montana Board of Pardons:

State of Montana
Board of Pardons and Parole
1002 Hollenbeck Road
Deer Lodge, Montana 59722
406-846-1404
Fax: 406-846-3512
http://mt.gov/bopp

Additional Information
Legal consequences as a result of the conviction are removed once a person is pardoned. According to Montana Code Ann. 46-23-301(b), "Pardon means a declaration of record that an individual is to be relieved of all legal consequences of a prior conviction."

Evidence of Exemplary Conduct
The Montana pardon application requests evidence of good conduct at the bottom of the application's first page: "Give a summary of your social history and accomplishments that qualify you for Executive Clemency."

Nebraska

Executive Clemency
Nebraska Constitution IV, Section 13

> Clemency in Nebraska is in the form of commutations, reprieves, pardons, remission of fines and forfeiture, and respites. It is the Nebraska State Board of Pardons that has executive clemency power including the power to grant pardons.

Eligibility
According to the Nebraska Board of Pardons, people with felonies will only be considered for a pardon 10 years after completion of a sentence. There is a three year wait for people with misdemeanors.

Contact Information

Nebraska Board of Pardons
P.O. Box 94754
Lincoln, Nebraska 68509-4754
402-479-5726
Applications may also be obtained from the Web site:
www.pardons.state.ne.us/content/new-application.pdf

Additional Information
According to the Nebraska Board of Pardons' "Frequently Asked Questions," the pardon returns the following lost civil rights:

- The right to go to professional schools.
- The right to bear arms.
- The right to vote, serve on a jury and hold public office.
- The right to take the civil service test.
- The right to obtain a passport.
- The right to obtain certain license.
- The right to enlist in the armed forces.

For more information visit the Web site at www.pardons.state.ne.us/faq.html.

Evidence of Exemplary Conduct
The Nebraska pardon application says, "Give your reason for requesting a pardon."

NEVADA

Executive Clemency
Nevada Constitution Article V, Section 14

> Clemency authority rests with the Nevada Pardons Board. The board is comprised of members of the Nevada Supreme Court, the Nevada attorney general, and the governor. The board grants pardons, commutes sentences and remits fines.

Eligibility
According to pardon instructions titled Community Case Application, individuals may apply for pardon once their sentence is completed. In addition, the board expects "a significant period of time" to pass before an application is considered.

Contact Information
To receive a pardon application mail your request to the Nevada Board of Pardons Commissioners:

Board of Pardons Commissioners
1445 Old Hot Springs Road #108B
Carson, Nevada 89711
775-687-8278
www.pardons.nv.gov

Additional Information
The pardon does not do the following:

- Overturn a conviction
- Erase a conviction
- Eliminate the registration of a sex offender
- Restore rights lost outside Nevada

Source: Nevada Board of Pardons

Evidence of Exemplary Conduct

The evidence of exemplary conduct request is revealed at the end of section one on the Nevada pardon application: "Have any extraordinary circumstances occurred that would merit the consideration and granting of a pardon?"

NEW HAMPSHIRE

Executive Clemency
New Hampshire Constitution Part 2, Article 52

> The governor has the power to grant pardons with the
> advice from the New Hampshire Executive Council.
> The remission of fines or forfeiture in criminal cases,
> however, is not part of the governor's executive clemency
> power.

Eligibility
Individuals convicted out-of-state or with federal convictions are
ineligible (Love, 2005).

Contact Information

Office of the Attorney General
New Hampshire Department of Justice
33 Capitol Street
Concord, New Hampshire 03301-6397
603-271-3658
Fax: 603-271-2110
http://doj.nh.gov

Additional Information
The New Hampshire attorney general's office is in charge of processing
pardon applications. New Hampshire Pardon and Parole Laws, RSA
4:21. The New Hampshire attorney general's office will contact the
following:

- The sentencing judge in the applicant's case
- The prosecutor in the applicant's case

Also, the office will obtain the criminal records check of the applicant
from the New Hampshire State Police.

The victim connected to the case will also be contacted and the
victim's response to the pardon application will be obtained from the
prosecutor.

Evidence of Exemplary Conduct

The New Hampshire application simply states, "Give a brief statement of the reason why you want a pardon."

NEW JERSEY

Executive Clemency
New Jersey Constitution Article V, Section 2

> The governor has the sole authority to grant reprieves, pardons, commutations, and also has the power to restore civil rights.

Eligibility
No requirements. Incarcerated individuals may also apply. Source: New Jersey State Parole Board.

Contact Information
To receive a pardon application mail your request to the New Jersey State Parole Board:

New Jersey State Parole Board
P.O. Box 862
Trenton, New Jersey 08625-0862
609-292-4257
Fax: 609-943-4769
www.nj.gov/parole

Additional Information
The Parole Board issues Certificates of Good Conduct, New Jersey Administrative Code 10A § 70-8.2, which helps the offender obtain employment and prevents licensing agencies from disqualifying an individual because of a criminal record. The certificate is not a pardon and does not forgive an offense. The individual must have been paroled by the board to be eligible.

Evidence of Exemplary Conduct
Two sentences sum up the exemplary conduct questions in the New Jersey application. The first sentence asks, "What is your reason for seeking clemency?" The second sentence says, "State briefly why you believe you should be granted clemency?"

NEW MEXICO

Executive Clemency
New Mexico Constitution Article V, Section 6

> Pardon authority is the responsibility of the governor. The governor may also grant reprieves, conditional release, and commutation of sentence for people incarcerated. Formerly incarcerated persons, however, may only apply for a pardon (pardon to restore civil rights).

Eligibility
In the New Mexico Executive Clemency Guidelines, before a pardon application is considered, a person who is convicted of a felony must wait a certain amount of years:

- Convicted of a fourth-degree felony, a person must wait five years after completion of a sentence
- Convicted of a third-degree felony, a person must wait six years after completion of a sentence
- Convicted of a second-degree felony, a person must wait seven years after completion of parole
- Convicted of a first-degree felony, a person must wait eight years after completion of parole

Contact Information
To receive a pardon application contact the governor:

Pardon/Paroles
Office of the Governor
State Capitol Building
Santa Fe, New Mexico 87501
505-476-2200

Applications may also be obtained from the governor's Web site:
www.governor.state.nm.us/pardon.php?mm=6

Evidence of Exemplary Conduct
The evidence of exemplary conduct request is found in the New Mexico Governor's Executive Clemency Guidelines:

To assist the recommending authorities in the evaluation process, applicants should include any significant achievements, such as employment and educational accomplishments; provide evidence of good citizenship and details about charitable and civic activities or other contributions made to the community.

NEW YORK

Executive Clemency
New York Constitution Article IV, Section 4

> The New York Constitution states that clemency gives the governor the power to grant reprieves, pardons, and commutations. Pardons are only granted when no other legal remedy is available. In New York, there are two legal remedies available: Certificate of Good Conduct and Certificate of Relief.

Certificate Eligibility
Once all the necessary documents are included in the application a representative will conduct an interview. The New York Board of Parole will determine if a certificate is warranted and determine which disability will be removed.

Certificate of Relief from Disabilities
- Issued to those with misdemeanors and one felony
- Not issued if a person has more than one felony
- Granted by the sentencing court

Certificate of Good Conduct
People with more than one felony are eligible for the Certificate of Good Conduct after several years of crime free living. The New York Board of Parole grants Certificate of Good Conduct. The eligibility requirements are the following:
- For a misdemeanor, a one year wait is required
- For a C, D, or E felony, a three year wait is required
- For an A, or B felony, a five year wait is required

Source: New York State Division of Parole.

Pardon Contact Information
To request an application for a certificate write to the Executive Department:

State of New York
Executive Department
Division of Parole
Certificate Review Unit
97 Central Avenue
Albany, New York 12206
(518) 485-8953
For more information and to obtain either certificate, consult
the Division of Parole frequently asked questions:
http://parole.state.ny.us/FAQs.asp

North Carolina

Executive Clemency
North Carolina Constitution Article III, Section 5(6)

> The governor has authority to grant pardons and commutations.

Pardon Eligibility
A five-year wait after completion of the sentence is required. Source: Governor's Clemency Office.

Pardon Contact Information
To receive a pardon application write to the Governor's Clemency Office:

Governor's Clemency Office
4294 Mail Service Center
Raleigh, North Carolina 27699-4294
919-715-1695
Fax: 919-715-8623
For more information visit the Web site:
www.doc.state.nc.us/clemency/glossary.htm

Additional Information
The Office of Executive Clemency Web site states that there are three kinds of pardons:

- Pardon of Forgiveness—the individual's crime is forgiven.
- Pardon of Innocence—the individual's charges are dismissed.
- Unconditional Pardon—restores firearm rights to the individual.

The criminal record is not expunged by the pardon. Only the judicial branch can expunge a record according to the North Carolina General Statutes §§ 15A-145, 146 and 149.

NORTH DAKOTA

Executive Clemency
North Dakota Constitution Article V, Section 7

> The governor grants pardons, reprieves, and commutations.

Eligibility
No requirements. Source: Pardon Advisory Board.

Contact Information
To receive a pardon application contact the North Dakota Pardon Advisory Board:

North Dakota Pardon Advisory Board
PO Box 5521
Bismarck, North Dakota 58506-5521
701-328-6190
Fax: 701-328-6186
www.nd.gov/docr/parole/advisory.html

Additional Information
According to information from the North Dakota Advisory Board, the pardon application will be reviewed in two stages: once by the Pardon Advisory Board and second by the governor's representative. The board may also decide to interview the applicant. After the investigation, the board will send the governor a recommendation for or against pardon consideration.

Evidence of Exemplary Conduct
Applicants must discuss evidence of good conduct by thoroughly answering the question on the North Dakota pardon application that says, "Tell us what is the reason/justification for your request. Be specific as to your reason(s) for relief."

OHIO

Executive Clemency
Ohio Constitution Article III, Section 11

> The governor of the state of Ohio has the sole authority to grant executive clemency in the form of pardon, commutation, and reprieve.

Eligibility
No time requirement is set for applying for a pardon in Ohio. Source: Ohio Parole Board.

Contact Information
To receive a pardon application contact the Ohio Parole Board:

Ohio Parole Board
Clemency Section
770 West Broad Street
Columbus, Ohio 43222
614-752-1200
1-888-344-1441
A pardon application may also be obtain in PDF format:
www.drc.state.oh.us/web/ExecClemency.htm

Additional Information
A pardon takes away the difficulties of the criminal record. According to the Ohio Revised Code 2967.04 (B), "An unconditional pardon relieves the person to whom it is granted of all disabilities arising out of the conviction or convictions from which it is granted."

Evidence of Exemplary Conduct
The Ohio Parole Board Application for Executive Clemency Instructions and Guidelines encourages the applicant to list involvement in activities:

> Please indicate any participation in activities including volunteer work that demonstrates efforts to give back to the community. If incarcerated, please describe any

programming or work assignments that demonstrate assistance to other inmates or members of the public (e.g. tutor, community services projects, etc.).

OKLAHOMA

Executive Clemency
Oklahoma Constitution Article IV, Section 10

> The governor has the authority to grant pardons, reprieves, and commutations in Oklahoma.

Eligibility
A person is eligible to apply for a pardon once the sentence is discharged, or if on supervision, the supervision must be for at least five consecutive years according to the Oklahoma General Counsel.

Contact Information
To receive a pardon application contact the Oklahoma General Counsel:

General Counsel
Attn: Pardons
First National Center
120 North Robinson Avenue, Suite 900 West
Oklahoma City, Oklahoma 73102-7436
405-602-5863
Fax: 405-602-6437
www.ppb.state.ok.us

Additional Information
The pardon does not expunge the record, but a non-violent first-offender who is granted a full pardon may petition the court for expungement no later than 10 years after receiving the pardon. Oklahoma Statutes Title 22, Chapter 1 § 18(7).

Evidence of Exemplary Conduct
The evidence of good conduct request is found on the pardon application under the heading "Charitable and Community Activities." Applicants are encouraged to list contributions to the community:

> Describe any charitable or civic activities in which you have been engaged, or other contributions you have made to the community, since your conviction. In this

regard, you may include the names of any organizations in which you have participated, the time periods of you participation, your role in these activities.

OREGON

Executive Clemency
Oregon Constitution Article V, Section 14

> The governor has the authority to grant commutations, remissions of fines, pardons, and reprieves.

Eligibility
The Oregon Information on Applications for Executive Clemency states that one must demonstrate "rehabilitation" in the way that one talks and lives because pardons are only granted in "exceptional" situations.

Contact Information
To receive a pardon application contact the governor:

Governor of Oregon
900 Court Street, North East
Salem, Oregon 97301-4047
503-378-4582
Fax: 503-378-6827
http://governor.oregon.gov

Additional Information
The Oregon Information on Applications for Executive Clemency reminds people to provide any additional information necessary to help the governor make a decision concerning the application. In other words, include any documentation that enhances worthiness for pardon consideration. There are other factors to keep in mind:

- The completed pardon process may take six months to finalize.
- Pardon applicants who have convictions that can be "set aside" or expunged by the court will not be considered for pardon. For more information about the qualifications for judicial expungement consult Oregon Revised Statutes 137.225.

Exemplary Conduct

Question 11 on the Oregon clemency application reveals the exemplary conduct request: "Tell about your involvement with any public service or community activities. List any special accomplishments."

PENNSYLVANIA

Executive Clemency
Pennsylvania Constitution Article IV, Section 9(a)

> The governor has the power to grant executive clemency in the form of pardons, commutation of sentence, reprieves, and remission of fines and forfeiture. A pardon cannot be granted except after recommendation from the Pennsylvania Board of Pardons.

Eligibility
Some of the factors the Pennsylvania board considers in a pardon application include the following:

1. Has all court requirements been met?
2. Has the applicant rehabilitated his or her life?
3. Has enough time passed since the ending of the sentence?

For more information on what the board will consider in a pardon application visit the Board of Pardons Web site and see "Eligibility."

Contact Information
To receive a pardon application contact the Pennsylvania Board of Pardons:

Pennsylvania Board of Pardons
333 Market Street, 15th Floor
Harrisburg, Pennsylvania 17126-0333
717-787-2596
Fax: 717-772-3135
For more information visit the Web site:
http://sites.state.pa.us/PA_Exec/BOP

Additional Information
According to the Pennsylvania Board of Pardons, after a five year waiting period, an individual who has a summary offense may request his or her record expunged by the Court of Common Please without applying for a pardon. House Bill 1543 (Act 134). The bill went into effect on January 26, 2009. Summary offenses are minor crimes such as disorderly conduct, first offense shoplifting, harassment, underage drinking, and violations of the Motor Vehicle Code.

Rhode Island

Executive Clemency
Rhode Island Constitution Article IX, Section 13

> The governor has authority to grant pardons and reprieves.

Eligibility
No restrictions. Rhode Island General Laws § 13-10-1.

Contact Information
For more information write to the governor:

Office of the Governor
State House, Room 115
Providence, Rhode Island 02903
401-222-2080
www.governor.ri.gov

Additional Information
In Rohde Island, there is no official pardon application. The Deputy Executive Counsel's instructions state that individuals requesting a pardon must gather the necessary documentation including the following:

- The applicant's Bureau of Criminal Identification Report
- Description of the offenses
- Conduct during parole period or incarceration
- Any police reports connected to the crime or crimes
- Any additional documentation that may encourage pardon consideration

Evidence of Exemplary Conduct
The Deputy Executive Counsel's instruction for applying for a pardon says, "Any other information that the applicant believes would be helpful in a determination (for example, letters of support and a description of unique personal circumstances that would warrant a pardon)."

SOUTH CAROLINA

Executive Clemency
South Carolina Constitution Article IV, Section 14

> It is the South Carolina Board of Probation, Parole and
> Pardon Services that has the authority to grant pardons.
> The governor commutes a sentence and issues reprieves.

Eligibility
Once an individual's sentence is complete or discharged and all court
fines are paid, an application for pardon may be submitted. South
Carolina Code Ann. § 24-21-950 (A)(1).

Contact Information
To receive a pardon application contact the South Carolina Pardon
Services:

> Department of Probation, Parole, and Pardon Services
> Attn: Legal Services, Pardon Application Processing
> 2221 Devine Street, Suite 600
> P.O. Box 50666
> Columbia, South Carolina 29250
> 803-734-9220
> Fax: 803-734-9440
> Applications may also be obtained in PDF format:
> www.dppps.sc.gov/apply_for_a_pardon.html

Additional Information
According to the Probation, Parole and Pardon Services instructions,
the following will occur as a result of the pardon:

1. The right to participate in jury service and hold public office is
   restored by pardon.
2. The pardon will not expunge the criminal record.
3. The application process may take seven to nine months to complete.
4. The pardon will allow a person to be licensed for any occupation
   that requires a license.
5. The pardon will not relieve one the responsibility of registering
   as a sex offender.

SOUTH DAKOTA

Executive Clemency
South Dakota Constitution Article IV, Section 3

> South Dakota's clemency is in the form of commutation, pardon, remission of fine or forfeiture, and reprieve. The governor has sole authority to grant clemency including pardons with recommendation from the South Dakota Board of Pardons and Paroles.

Eligibility
A five year wait is required for first-time offenders. Source: South Dakota Codified Laws Chapter 24-14-8.

Contact Information

South Dakota Board of Pardons and Paroles
P.O. Box 5911
Sioux Falls, South Dakota 57117
605-367-5040
Fax: 605-367-5115
Applications may also be acquired from the Web site:
http://doc.sd.gov/forms

Additional Information
Pardon records can be sealed according to South Dakota Law:

> Upon the granting of a pardon under the provisions of this chapter, the Governor shall order that all official records relating to the pardoned person's arrest, indictment or information, trial, finding of guilt, application for a pardon, and the proceedings of the Board of Pardons and Paroles shall be sealed. South Dakota Codified Laws 24-14-11.

Evidence of Exemplary Conduct

The South Dakota pardon application evidence of exemplary conduct request requires that the applicant create a personal plea letter asking why the pardon is wanted. The application says, "The letter should describe what debilitating effects the conviction is causing such as limiting employment and how clemency will benefit you and society."

The application also says, "List all honors, awards or achievements you have accomplished since your conviction."

TENNESSEE

Executive Clemency
Tennessee Constitution Article III, Section 6

> Clemency in Tennessee is granted by the governor and is in the form of pardon, commutation, reprieve, and exoneration. Exoneration occurs when the conviction is removed from the record.

Eligibility
A five year crime free wait after the completion of a sentence is required before an applicant will be considered for a pardon. Source: Tennessee Board of Probation and Parole.

Contact Information
To receive a pardon application contact the Tennessee Board of Probation and Parole:

> State of Tennessee
> Board of Probation and Parole
> 404 James Robertson Parkway, Suite 1300
> Nashville, Tennessee 37243-0850
> 615-741-1150
> You may also fax your request:
> 615-741-5337
> www.tn.gov/bopp/home.htm

Additional Information
According to the pardon application instructions, the requestor must attach a cover letter to the front of the application and indicate what type of relief she or he desires:

> I request a pardon for my _____conviction that will allow me to enter the_____ occupation.

Evidence of Exemplary Conduct
The evidence of exemplary conduct request is actually part of the governor's criteria for pardon consideration found immediately on

the first page of the Tennessee Board of Probation and Parole pardon application: "Petitioner has the obligation to provide written verification of good citizenship and of compelling and specific need..."

Simone R. Richardson

TEXAS

Executive Clemency
Texas Constitution Article IV, Section 11(b)

> The governor has the power to grant clemency in Texas with recommendation from the Board of Pardons and Paroles. Executive clemency in Texas is in the form of commutation of sentence, conditional and full pardons, and reprieves for medical reasons.

Eligibility
A person may apply for a pardon in Texas once the sentence is completed. Source: Texas Administrative Code Title 37, Part 5 § 143.5.

Contact Information
To receive a pardon application contact the Texas Board of Pardons:

Texas Board of Pardons and Paroles
Clemency Section
8610 Shoal Creek Boulevard
Austin, Texas 78757
512-406-5852
Fax: 512-467-0945
An application may also be obtained from the Web site:
www.tdcj.state.tx.us/bpp
See "Clemency."

Additional Information
According to the Texas Code of Criminal Procedure Article 55.01 (a) (1)(B), a person who received a conviction of a felony or misdemeanor may have the files expunged if pardoned.

Evidence of Exemplary Conduct
The evidence of exemplary conduct request in the Texas pardon application is found in section E titled Justification for Clemency Consideration. The application says, "What have you done since your conviction(s) to show that you deserve full pardon and restoration of civil rights consideration, including rehabilitative efforts that you have made?"

UTAH

Executive Clemency
Utah Constitution Article VII, Section 12

> It is the responsibility of the Utah Board of Pardons and Paroles to grant full and unconditional pardons. The process of remission of fines and forfeiture and the commutation of a sentence is also the authority of the board. The governor grants reprieves and respites. What is a respite?

Respite
If an incarcerated person needs medical treatment, the individual will be released temporarily for medical reasons. The short-term release is called a respite.

Eligibility
According to the Utah Administrative Code R671-315-1, a five year wait after sentence is completed is required.

Contact Information
To receive a pardon application contact the Utah Board of Pardons:

Utah Board of Pardons and Parole
448 East 6400 South, Suite 300
Murray, Utah 84107
801-261-6464
Fax: 801-261-6481
www.bop.utah.gov

Evidence of Exemplary Conduct
The exemplary conduct request says, "In a separate letter which must accompany the application, state the extenuating circumstances supporting the basis for the pardon request."

The important phrase in the above line is "extenuating circumstances supporting." In other words, the applicant must provide supporting evidence to help enhance pardon consideration. The applicant may provide the evidence such as good deeds, volunteer activity, educational fulfillment, vocational training, and evidence of barriers to certain employment.

VERMONT

Executive Clemency
Vermont Constitution Chapter II, Section 20

> The power to grant a pardon rests with the governor. The governor's decision is final. There is no appeal process. The governor also remits fines and grants reprieves.

Eligibility
The Governor's Guidelines for Pardon Consideration say that a ten year wait after conviction is required.

Contact Information
To receive a pardon application contact the following:

Pardon Coordinator
Office of the Governor
109 State Street, The Pavilion
Montpelier, Vermont 05609-0101
802-828-3333
Fax: 802-828-3339
http://governor.vermont.gov

Additional Information
In the Governor's Guidelines for Pardon Consideration, the applicant must satisfy three important criteria:

1. The applicant must demonstrate that the pardon will benefit society in some way (not the applicant).
2. The applicant must reveal exemplary conduct since the conviction.
3. The applicant must show that the pardon will remove barriers to employment.

Evidence of Exemplary Conduct
The evidence of good conduct request in the Vermont pardon application says, "Petitioners must demonstrate a substantial period of good citizenship and an exemplary life since conviction. Please indicate examples of constructive conduct and specific achievements, if any (attach a separate sheet if more space is needed)."

VIRGINIA

Executive Clemency
Virginia Constitution Article V, Section 12

> Only the governor has the power to grant pardons and the restoration of civil rights.

Eligibility
According to the secretary of the commonwealth of Virginia, a five year wait after completion of a sentence is required to apply for a simple pardon. In addition, to be considered for a pardon, a convicted felon must first have rights restored by the governor. For more information visit the Web site:

www.commonwealth.virginia.gov/JudicialSystem/Clemency/
simplePardon.cfm

Contact Information
To receive a pardon application contact the following:

Clemency Specialist
Office of the Secretary of the Commonwealth
Post Office Box 2454
Richmond, Virginia 23218-2454
804-692-2542
www.commonwealth.virginia.gov/JudicialSystem/index.cfm

For Restoration of Civil Rights

Restoration of Rights Director
Office of the Secretary of the Commonwealth
Post Office Box 2454
Richmond, Virginia 23218-2454
804-692-2531

Evidence of Exemplary Conduct
In Virginia there is no official pardon application to fill out. The applicant must provide evidence of exemplary conduct in a letter to the

governor and explain why the pardon is desired. For more information about what to include in the letter visit the Web site of the secretary of the commonwealth of Virginia.

WASHINGTON

Executive Clemency
Washington Constitution Article III, Section 9.

> The governor has the power to grant pardons, commute a sentence, and grant reprieves. The governor also has the power to return the offender's right to hold public office, vote, and possess a firearm (firearm rights are rarely restored).

Eligibility
In a letter from the office of the governor, ex-offenders with convictions occurring out-of-state or federal convictions need to submit an application for restoration of civil rights before the Washington Board of Clemency and Pardons.

Contact Information
To receive a pardon application contact the governor:

Office of the Governor
P.O. Box 40002
Olympia, Washington 98504-0002
360-753-6780
www.governor.wa.gov
Or visit:
www.cjpf.org/clemency/WashingtonApp.pdf

Additional Information
Information from the office of the governor reads, "Please note that a pardon does not erase a conviction but merely excuses the punishment imposed by the sentencing court."

Evidence of Exemplary Conduct
The exemplary conduct request in the Washington pardon application says, "Describe what you have done to demonstrate your rehabilitation: (For example, list employment/education history; if restitution was ordered, has restitution been made?)."

See appendix D for more information on the pardon procedure in the state of Washington.

WEST VIRGINIA

Executive Clemency
West Virginia Constitution Article VII, Section 11.

> The governor has the authority to grant pardons, reprieves, remit fines, and to commute a sentence in West Virginia. The governor may also grant a medical respite. A respite means to be release from incarceration temporarily for medical reasons.

Eligibility
Pardons are granted only to state ex-offenders (Love, 2005).

Contact Information
To receive a pardon application contact the governor:

Office of Governor
General Counsel
1900 Kanawha Boulevard, East
Charleston, West Virginia 25305
304-558-2000
1-888-438-2731
www.wvgov.org

Additional Information
West Virginia law permits a person who receives a full pardon to apply to the courts for expungement of a criminal record. Chapter 5 § 5-1-16a of the West Virginia Code:

> Any person who has received a full and unconditional pardon from the governor, pursuant to the provisions of section eleven, article VII of the constitution of West Virginia and section sixteen of this article, may petition the circuit court in the county were the conviction was had to have the record of such conviction expunged.

Evidence of Exemplary Conduct

The West Virginia pardon application evidence of exemplary conduct request requires applicants to describe positive activity involvement since incarceration:

> If you are no longer incarcerated for the above offense(s) please describe employment, education, community and family activities that you have accomplished since your conviction, and all other information you feel is pertinent to consideration for Executive Clemency.

WISCONSIN

Executive Clemency
Wisconsin Constitution Article V, Section 6

> The governor has sole authority to grant pardons with a recommendation from the Governor's Advisory Board. The governor also grants reprieves and commutations after conviction.

Eligibility
The executive clemency information from the office of the governor states that a person (convicted felon) interested in a pardon must wait five years after completing a sentence to apply. If a person is not eligible under the current guideline the individual may fill out an Eligibility Rule Waiver form.

Contact Information
To receive a pardon application contact the governor:

Office of the Governor
Pardon Advisory Board
Room 115 East
State Capitol
P.O. Box 7863
Madison, Wisconsin 53707
608-266-1212
www.wisgov.state.wi.us
An application may also be obtained from the Web site:
www.wi-doc.com/index_adult.htm

Evidence of Exemplary Conduct
The application instructions for executive clemency reveal the evidence of exemplary conduct request on line 15: "Explain why you need clemency in your own words—what your plans are, how you have changed, why you feel you deserve this extraordinary privilege, etc."

WYOMING

Executive Clemency

Wyoming Constitution Article IV, Section 5

> The governor has the authority to grant pardons, reprieves, remit fines and forfeiture, and grant commutations. The Wyoming Parole Board has authority to grant restoration of voting rights.

Eligibility

According to a letter I received from C.A. Crofts, counsel to the governor, the governor prefers that an individual wait ten years after completion of the sentence before applying for a pardon.

Contact Information

To receive a pardon application contact the governor:

Office of the Governor
State Capitol, Room 124
Cheyenne, Wyoming 82002-0010
330-777-7434
Fax: 307-632-3909
http://governor.wy.gov

To receive an application for restoration of voting rights contact the Wyoming Board of Parole:

Board of Parole
3120 Old Faithful Road, Suite 100
Cheyenne, Wyoming 82002
307-777-5444
Restoration of voting rights applications may
also be obtained from the Web site:
http://boardofparole.wy.gov

Additional Information

More information on the application process may be found in the Wyoming Statutes Ann. § 7-13-803.

Information on what to include in the pardon application may be found in the Wyoming Statutes Ann. § 7-13-804.

CHAPTER 10

INCENTIVES TO HIRE EX-OFFENDERS

The Work Opportunity Tax Credit (WOTC) and the Federal Bonding Program are two incentives implemented by the federal government to encourage employers to hire formerly incarcerated persons and other citizens in need of work experience.

WORK OPPORTUNITY TAX CREDIT

The Work Opportunity Tax Credit is a tax credit given to businesses who hire citizens from certain groups. The credit is designed to increase employment opportunities to individuals who fall under the following 12 target categories according to the Department of Labor:

- Vocational rehabilitation referral
- SSI Recipient
- Unemployed veteran
- Disconnected youth
- Designated community resident
- SNAP (Supplemental Nutrition Assistance Program) recipient
- TANF (Temporary Assistance to Needy Families) recipient (long term)
- Summer youth

- Ex-felon
- Other TANF recipient
- Veteran
- Hurricane Katrina employee

The WOTC stipulates, however, that the formerly incarcerated person must be a "qualified ex-felon." Other than having the proper job skills for the job, the Department of Labor defines a qualified ex-felon:

> Ex-felon—individual who was convicted of a felony and who is hired not more than one year after the conviction or release from prison.

The Department of Labor reports that businesses can earn $9,000 per new long-term TANF recipient employed over a two year period.

HOW DOES IT WORK?

A. An employer may participate in WOTC by first obtaining IRS Form 8850 Prescreening Notice and Certification Request for the Work Opportunity Tax Credit.

B. On the day individual is offered the job page one of 8850 is completed. After the individual is hired page two of 8850 is completed.

C. According to the Department of Labor, the employer must also fill out either ETA (Employment and Training Administration) form 9062 or 9061.

D. The completed forms are then mailed, within 28 days after the employee's hire date, to the state workforce agency's WOTC coordinator.

For more information, including any changes in the rule, concerning WOTC consult the following Web sites:

United States Department of Labor Employment and Training Administration (ETA)
www.doleta.gov/business/Incentives/opptax

Internal Revenue Service
www.irs.gov
Keywords: "Work Opportunity Tax Credit."

FEDERAL BONDING INSURANCE

The U.S. Department of Labor sponsors the Federal Bonding Program (also called a Fidelity Bond) which is business insurance issued free to employers and is designed to protect companies from any potential destruction of the business initiated by an employee with a not-so-hot background.

The Federal Bond is necessary because some employers are reluctant to hire ex-offenders and consider the formerly incarcerated an "at-risk" applicant—someone who can cause damage such as theft, embezzlement or forgery.

The bonding program protects the employer with business insurance coverage of $5000 and sometimes more depending on the company.

People who are self-employed do not qualify for the bond. Also, the bond does not cover accidents on the job or inadequate work of the employee.

HOW DOES IT WORK?

Either the employer or employee requests a bond from the nearest One-Stop Career Center or whichever agency is certified by the Federal Bonding Program in the employer's state. There is no special or lengthy paperwork to fill out nor is there an application to sign. The Federal Bond is issued to the employer immediately once the employee starts working.

Individuals eligible for the Federal Bonding Program include the following:

A. People with poor credit history

B. Veterans with dishonorable discharge

C. Ex-felons

D. Recovering addicts

E. People with little or no work history

For more information on the Federal Bonding Program visit www.
bonds4jobs.com.

The Ohio Department of Rehabilitation and Correction coordinates
the Federal Bonding Program for Ohio.

Ohio's eligibility criteria require the following:

- The position must be full-time
- The employee's criminal record must be verified
- The individual must not be self-employed

For more information about Ohio's bonding criteria visit
www.drc.ohio.gov/web/OJL_bonding.htm.

YOUR EFFORTS BENEFIT THE WORLD: MY MESSAGE TO THE EX-OFFENDER

A pardon is not guaranteed. So what happens if your efforts and your
hard work (exemplary conduct) and your gathering of information
and supporting documents result in your application being denied?
Perseverance is the key. State pardon agencies will include a timeframe
in which to reapply. Brush yourself off and pick yourself up. When the
time is right apply for the pardon again.

Failure to receive a pardon should not cause you suffering because
if you followed the steps necessary to apply for the pardon you have
already benefitted the world. By benefitting the world I mean you
unknowingly enhanced the well-being of others.

In other words, because of your efforts the following benefits will
transpire:

- **Your immediate family benefits**. Your mother and
  father, sister and brother, will talk with pride and joy

when your name is mentioned. The family's suffering, pain, worry and stress is finally over (incarceration and conviction affects the whole family). Emotional and mental healing can begin. Happiness and well-being will flourish.

- **Your children benefit**. Your children will see the great effort you put into improving your life and their lives, and your effort may encourage your children to do the same.

- **Your community benefits**. You become a tax paying citizen by acquiring employment. You will contribute to a whole host of programs to help your community and society.

- **Other people benefit**. You can help provide opportunities and assistance for others by volunteering for a nonprofit (or creating your own volunteer project). The opportunities and assistance may enhance many families thereby creating a domino effect of hope and prosperity that enhances the community, the state, the nation, and eventually the world.

We are all interconnected.

"All the knowledge that you ever want to discover is found at your local public library."

Simone R. Richardson

About the Author

When Simone R. Richardson decided to devote her life to work in the public library setting, her outlook on life changed when someone came up to Simone and said, "Ma'am, I've just been released from prison and I need help." Simone discovered the great need for resources for the ex-offender. Simone's contact with formerly incarcerated persons, and individuals with felony offenses, inspired her to develop a job search resource guide for ex-offenders for her library.

Simone acquired deep understanding, wisdom, and compassion concerning the plight of the formerly incarcerated person through her research, her facilitation of library job search seminars, her past resume workshops, and her volunteer work with the homeless and ex-offenders.

Simone's compassion compelled her to develop resources that leave a positive impact on the lives of former offenders. The positive impact is evident in her latest work *Executive Clemency by Pardon: A Guide to Pardon Success.*

Simone has been working in the public library setting for over 20 years and currently works as a public library librarian in Akron, Ohio. Simone holds a MLS degree from Kent State University.

BIBLIOGRAPHY

Community Legal Aid Service. "Expungement." Informational leaflet. Akron, OH, 2008.

Encyclopedia of Careers and Vocational Guidance. New York, NY: Ferguson, 2008.

Federal Bonding Program: A U.S. Department of Labor Initiative. "A Unique Job Placement Tool for the At-Risk Job Seeker." www. bonds4jobs.com. (accessed September 5, 2010).

Hayden, C.J. Get Hired Now. Berkeley, CA: Bay Tree, 2005.

Krannich, Ron. Best Jobs for Ex-Offenders: 101 Opportunities to Your New Life. Manassas, VA: Impact, 2009.

Love, Margaret Colgate. "Relief from the Collateral Consequences of a Criminal Conviction: A State-by-State Resource Guide." The Sentencing Project. www.sentencingproject.org/detail/publication. cfm?publication_id=115, June 2008.

National H.I.R.E. Network. "Federal Occupational Restrictions Affecting People with Criminal Records." www.hirenetwork.org/ fed_occ_restrictions.html (accessed September 5, 2010).

Ohio Department of Rehabilitation and Correction. "Federal Bonding Program."www.drc.ohio.gov/web/OJL_bonding.htm (accessed January 24, 2009).

Ohio Department of Rehabilitation and Correction. "Prisoner Community Service." www.drc.ohio.gov/web/commserv.htm (accessed January 21, 2009).

Ohio Legal Services. "Criminal Matters: Expungement." www. ohiolegalservices.org/ public/legal_problem/criminal-matters/ expungement/qandact_view (accessed December 23, 2009).

ONET: Dictionary of Occupational Titles. Indianapolis, IN: JIST Works, 2007. http://online.onetcenter.org.

Starting Fresh. Finding a Job with a Troubled Background. DVD. Jacksonville, FL: Linx Educational, 2007.

United States Bureau of Labor Statistics, U.S. Department of Labor, Occupational Outlook Handbook, 2008-09. Library Edition, Bulletin 2700. Washington, D.C.: U.S. Government Printing Office, 2008.

United States Department of Labor. "Work Opportunity Tax Credit." www. doleta.gov/business/Incentives/opptax (accessed September 6, 2010).

GLOSSARY

Amnesty
Amnesty is a form of clemency issued for the restoration of peace after political unrest. It is a kind of pardon that is given to a group of people for the same offense.

Commutation
The commutation is the shortening of a punishment to one less harsh. It is the reduction of a sentence. The commutation is a request to be released from incarceration by way of being eligible for parole at an earlier date, for instance.

Evidence of Exemplary Conduct (on a pardon application)
The evidence of exemplary conduct is the request on almost every pardon application that seeks information about accomplishments since the ending of the sentence.

Executive Clemency
Executive clemency is the constitutional power of the governor or president and is in the form of pardon, commutation, and reprieve. The commutation is the shortening of a punishment to one less harsh. The pardon restores rights lost as a result of the criminal conviction. The reprieve delays the carrying out of the sentence.

Exemplary Conduct
The good deeds an individual has achieved since the ending of his or her sentence.

Expungement
The conviction is removed from the person's record. An expungement, according to Ohio law, is the process of "sealing" a criminal record. Law enforcement officials may still review a sealed record if the individual has committed a crime.

Federal Bonding Insurance
www.bonds4jobs.com.
The U.S. Department of Labor sponsors the Federal Bonding Program which is business insurance issued free to employers. The insurance is designed to protect companies from any potential destruction of the business initiated by an employee with a not-so-hot background.

Federal Crimes
Only the president of the United States can pardon federal crimes. Some examples of federal crimes include the following:

Bank Robberies	Insurance Fraud
Bankruptcy Fraud	Jewelry and Gem Theft
Cargo Theft	Money Laundering
Hate Crime	Mortgage Fraud
Identity Theft	Telemarketing Fraud

Source: FBI "What We Investigate." *www.fbi.gov/hq.htm.*

Federal Employment Restrictions
Despite the fact that EEOC laws prohibit employment discrimination based solely on a conviction or arrest record, bars to employment still exist legally, especially on a federal level. It is important to know which jobs are prohibited for certain felonies. Some restrictions involve the following: care involving children, airport employment, health care, labor organizations, insurance, banking industry, and prisoner transport.

Informational Interview

The informational interview is called a nontraditional job search method. The informational interview is a part of networking for potential job leads. Instead of the employer interviewing you, you interview the employer.

Pardon

The pardon is not an expungement or sealing of a conviction but represents forgiveness of punishment and guilt. A candidate for pardon should have many years of living crime free. The pardon restores rights lost as a result of the criminal conviction.

Pardon Eligibility

The requirement needed to apply for a pardon.

Presidential Pardon

Presidential pardons are given to individuals who commit federal crimes. Only the president of the United States can grant presidential pardons. The pardon (in general) improves an individual's chances of obtaining licenses for jobs that were denied the pardon recipient because of his or her crimes.

Remission of Fine or Forfeiture

Remission of fine means one does not have to pay back a fine. Remission of forfeiture means the giving back of a person's property (and rights to property) that was taken away because of the conviction.

Reprieve

The reprieve usually applies to individuals on death-row. The reprieve request delays the carrying out of the sentence.

Respite

If an incarcerated person needs medical treatment, the individual will be released temporarily for medical reasons. The short-term release is called a respite.

United States Code
The United States Code is a compilation of federal laws.

Work Opportunity Tax Credit
www.doleta.gov/business/Incentives/opptax

The Work Opportunity Tax Credit is a tax credit given to businesses who hire citizens from certain groups. The credit is designed to increase employment opportunities to individuals who fall under 12 target categories:

- Vocational rehabilitation referral
- SSI Recipient
- Unemployed veteran
- Disconnected youth
- Designated community resident
- SNAP (Supplemental Nutrition Assistance Program) recipient
- TANF (Temporary Assistance to Needy Families) recipient (long term)
- Summer youth
- Ex-felon
- Other TANF recipient
- Veteran
- Hurricane Katrina employee

Appendix A

My Letter to the Honorable Dave Freudenthal, Governor of Wyoming (The first Governor to answer my letter)

Note: The concepts of Zen were removed from the book.

Simone Richardson

XXXXXXXX

XXXXXXXXX

June 14, 2008

The Honorable
Dave Freudenthal
Governor of Wyoming
200 West 24th Street
Cheyenne, Wyoming 82002-0010

Dear Governor Freudenthal:

I'm currently writing a book concerning executive clemency pardon. The goal of the resource is to encourage the formerly incarcerated to try this option as a way to relieve the stigma and bias surrounding a criminal record, as well as to try this option to enhance the ex-offender's credibility as a hardworking productive member of society.

The publisher of the book will be iUniverse, and it will probably be 100 to 150 pages long. The resource will be published in 2009. My recent published book, *The Zen of Resume Writing of Formerly Incarcerated Persons,* http://zenresumes.tripod.com, was published in May 2007.

My new book will also include concepts of Zen. I'm asking your permission to include in my book your brief answer, feelings, or thoughts to the following question:

> What three factors, characteristics, or qualities about an individual's pardon application prompts or encourages you to grant him or her a pardon?

I will make sure to cite you either before or after your response and recognize you in my acknowledgments. Your response received by July 7, 2008, will be greatly appreciated.

For your convenience I have enclosed a self addressed stamped envelope.

Sincerely,

Simone R. Richardson

Appendix B

My Response to C.A. Crofts, Counsel to the Honorable Dave Freudenthal Governor of Wyoming

Simone R. Richardson
XXXXXXXXX
XXXXXXXX

July 14, 2008

C.A. Crofts
Counsel to the Governor
Office of the Governor
State Capitol, Room 124
Cheyenne, Wyoming 82002-0010

Dear C.A. Crofts:

I want to take this opportunity to thank you and Governor Freudenthal for responding to my letter dated June 14, 2008, concerning Governor Freudenthal's brief answer, feelings, or thoughts to the question about the three factors the governor sees in a pardon application which compels him to grant a pardon.

What you wrote was exactly what I was looking for especially starting from the third paragraph which reads, "I can say that in general Governor Feudenthal will not even consider an application for pardon until ten years have passed…" You are letting people know (in Wyoming) what to strive for if they decide to take on this pardon challenge. I will thank you and the governor in the acknowledgement of my book.

It is clear from my pardon research that what is important is that the pardon seeker show some atonement for past crimes by giving back to the community, helping society in some way, or achieving educational advancement for the betterment of society and the world. Even the presidential pardon application information states that some of the factors that the president considers in the pardon application are the pardon seeker's participation in the community, activities in charity, and the seriousness of the applicant's crime.

As a librarian from Akron, Ohio, I encounter the formerly incarcerated almost every day. From what I have seen, most individuals want to live a good quality crime free life. I try to encourage them and tell them to never give up! I'm trying to do all I can, before I leave this earthly life, to put together resources to help the ex-offender achieve this goal. I was told by a coworker that helping ex-offenders was my ministry. Thank you for helping me in my quest!

With lovingkindness,

Simone R. Richardson

Appendix C

My Response Letter to the Office of the Honorable John Elias Baldacci, Governor of Maine, Addressed to Karla Black Deputy Legal Counsel

Simone Richardson
XXXXXXXX
XXXXXXXXX

November 12, 2008

Karla Black
Deputy Legal Counsel
State of Maine
Office of the Governor
1 State House Station
Augusta, Maine 04333-0001

Dear Ms. Black:

Thank you for responding to my inquiry concerning three factors, characteristics, or qualities about an individual's pardon application that prompts or encourages you (and Governor Baldacci) to grant him or her a pardon. You are helping me in my quest to change the world. I will acknowledge you and the Governor's Board of Executive Clemency in my book.

Every day I encounter and assist formerly incarcerated people in my profession as a librarian. Some of these people feel that they are facing a brick wall after applying for a job time and time again to no avail. Some want to give up but I tell them to "Never give up!"

My goal is to help the formerly incarcerated by revealing to them that by taking the necessary steps to improve their lives (e.g., obtaining vocational training, seeking higher education, doing community service, pursuing starting a business, creating a nonprofit that helps others, etc.), and then applying for a pardon will not only enhance their future but enhance the future of the community and thereby the world.

Even if the pardon does not materialize, I encourage former inmates to take self improvement steps anyway.

I have found that the simple action of showing compassion toward the formerly incarcerated changes them internally and then the positive transformation begins. Thanks again for all your assistance!

With lovingkindness,

Simone R. Richardson

Appendix D

Letter from the Office of the Governor State of Washington
(Reprinted by permission)

Simone R. Richardson

CHRISTINE O. GREGOIRE
Governor

STATE OF WASHINGTON

OFFICE OF THE GOVERNOR

P.O. Box 40002 • Olympia, Washington 98504-0002 • (360) 753-6780 • www.governor.wa.gov

March 23, 2009

Simone Richardson

XXXXXXXX

XXXXXXXX

Re: Board of Clemency and Pardons (Board)

Dear Ms. Richardson:

The power of the Governor to grant clemency to convicted felons is a great responsibility and is something that is taken very seriously.

Article III, Section 9 of the Washington Constitution gives the Governor exclusive power to grant clemency in Washington state. It is an awesome responsibility. The term "clemency" is a general term for a variety of different acts of grace. The Governor can delay implementation of a sentence (grant a reprieve), commute (reduce) a sentence, remove all punishment for a crime (grant a pardon), restore a felon's civil rights to vote (for example, when petitioner has not completed all sentence requirements such as legal financial obligations), hold public office, and own firearms, or commute a death sentence to life in prison. All of these powers reduce or eliminate punishment for a crime. The Governor does not have the power to expunge a criminal record; only the courts have that power.

Submission of a clemency petition (see enclosed form) is required for consideration. When a person files a clemency petition with the Governor, the petition is referred to the Board of Clemency and Pardons. The Board consists of five people appointed by the Governor and confirmed by the Senate. The Board's review committee examines all petitions for clemency/pardon and determines which petitions will be heard by the full board. The Board holds a hearing on those petitions selected by the review committee. At the hearing, the petitioner and his or her lawyer, if represented, and a few family members or character witnesses may advocate on behalf of the petition. The prosecutor of the county where the crime was committed as well as the victims and their families are also invited to speak.

After the testimony at the hearing, the Board votes on whether to recommend that the Governor grant clemency or deny the petition. There are no specific guidelines that bind the Board or the Governor in their decisions. Each Board member votes based on his or her own interpretation of the petition and life experiences. Statute provides that the Board "shall receive petitions and, *in*

150

Simone Richardson
March 23, 2009
Page 2

extraordinary cases, make recommendations to the Governor." The Governor, upon recommendation from the Board "may grant an extraordinary release for reasons of serious health problems, senility, advanced age, extraordinary meritorious acts, or other extraordinary circumstances." The Governor is free to place conditions on a pardon, such as not committing any further crimes or never possessing a firearm.

Once the petition is on the Governor's desk with a positive recommendation from the Board, she reviews the full case in great detail. Only when she is convinced that she fully understands the circumstances of the crime and the reasons for the petition does she make her final decision. Please understand that the Governor grants clemency or pardon in only the most rare and exceptional of circumstances.

The enclosed document is the necessary form to petition for clemency or pardon in the state of Washington. Because of the very large number of requests, and due to our limited staff, the burden falls on the person requesting the action to provide the information and documents that demonstrate a compelling justification. Accordingly, please complete the enclosed petition and return the **original petition and three complete sets of all materials** to be submitted for review to Terri Gottberg, Office of the Attorney General, PO Box 40116, Olympia, WA 98504.

The Board of Clemency and Pardons' review committee reviews all pending requests for clemency/pardon and determines which petitions will be heard by the full Board. The Board will review only those cases referred by the review committee and will make a positive recommendation to the Governor only in the most extraordinary cases. Only after the Board has determined whether to review an application and has made a recommendation to the Governor will she evaluate the case for possible executive action. The Governor may or may not accept the Board's recommendation.

The Board, by itself, has the power to restore civil rights for federal and out-of-state felons *except* for the right to possess firearms. Restoration of firearms rights requires personal action by the Governor through her pardon power. To date, the Governor has rarely restored firearms rights— and in fact has specifically *not* restored those rights in most pardons granted. Requests for restoration of the right to possess firearms are treated the same as any other request for clemency. Again, I must advise you that positive action can rarely be expected. The Federal government, Division of Alcohol, Tobacco, and Firearms has the power to restore firearms rights. However, we understand that Congress has barred them from doing so.

To assist you in determining whether an application for clemency or pardon is appropriate in this instance, please take note of the following policies of the Board:

1. Clemency or pardon is granted in only the most extraordinary of circumstances. It must be remembered that good institutional behavior and positive rehabilitative efforts during incarceration and following release are considered a basic expectation and do not warrant exceptionally meritorious status. However, this behavior will have an effect on good time earned

and, therefore, on a potential release date. Only in rare and exceptional instances do actions and the passage of time following conviction and sentencing make clemency or pardon a viable option.

2.   It is not the Board's function to reexamine or second-guess the decisions of the Indeterminate Sentence Review Board or to determine the propriety or fairness of indeterminate sentences as compared to standard range sentences. This is a matter already addressed by the judiciary and inappropriate for review by this Board.

3.   It is generally not the Board's function to re-litigate or second-guess the decision of a sentencing court. Additionally, the fairness or constitutionality of a particular statute or decision are not matters properly considered by this Board. Our judicial system offers guarantees and relief through its own comprehensive appeals process. Those who believe they have been unjustly convicted or sentenced are entitled to avail themselves of their right to appeal for judicial review.

4.   Petitions filed for serious health reasons must first be reviewed and processed by the Department of Corrections (DOC) according to their established medical protocol. Any such petitions must be accompanied by a DOC medical evaluation and positive recommendation signed by the Secretary of the Department of Corrections. The Board will not review any petitions not accompanied by a positive recommendation.

5.   If the Board finds no compelling justification or extraordinary circumstances to warrant a recommendation of clemency or pardon, it is the Board's policy to deny subsequent petitions unless there is substantial change in the facts from the prior petition.

Finally, please note that a pardon does **not** erase a conviction but merely excuses the punishment imposed by the sentencing court. The vacation of a criminal record must be obtained pursuant to RCW 9.94A.640. The procedure spelled out under that law requires application to the Superior Court that entered the conviction.

Sincerely,

XXXXXXXX
XXXXXXXX

Legal Affairs Coordinator

Enclosures

APPENDIX E

STATE OF MAINE PARDON
(Actual pardon certificate reprinted by permission)

Simone R. Richardson

STATE OF MAINE

The Governor of the State of Maine

WARRANT OF FULL AND FREE PARDON

TO ALL PERSONS to whom this **WARRANT OF FULL AND FREE PARDON** shall come, let it be known that:

was the accused in a criminal proceeding before the District Court, District 2, Division of Southern Aroostook, located at Houlton, entitled **STATE OF MAINE v.**   bearing Criminal Docket Number   In this proceeding on the 31st day of July, 1995,   was adjudged guilty of the crime of assault in violation of 17-A M.R.S.A. § 207(1) and (2) (1983 and Supp. 1994) (Class D) and was sentenced to a term of imprisonment of five (5) days in County Jail, all suspended, with a period of probation of one (1) year.

has petitioned this Governor for clemency.

WHEREFORE, upon full consideration of the facts previously stated, I do hereby grant   a **FULL AND FREE PARDON** respecting such criminal conviction, of which all are to take notice.

In testimony whereof, I have caused the Great Seal of the State of Maine to be hereunto affixed. Witness, our Governor, at the State House on this ____ day of May , 2010.

_____
Governor

_____
Secretary of State

154

Appendix F

Resources to Help Improve Skills

College Preparation
CLEP The College-Level Examination Program, Third Edition. New York, NY: Kaplan, 2008

GED
Princeton Review. Cracking the GED 2009 Edition. New York, NY: Random House, 2008.

Job and Career Opportunities
Krannich, Ron. Best Jobs for Ex-Offenders. Manassas Park, VA: Impact Publications, 2009.

Math Preparation
Basic Math & Pre-Algebra. New York: LearningExpress, 2007.

Parenting Skills
Stawar, Terry L. How to Be a Responsible Father: A Workbook for the Offender. Annapolis, MD: American Correctional Association, 2007.

Study Skills

Lorayne, Harry. Super Memory—Super Student: How to Raise Your Grades in 30 Days. Boston, MA: Little Brown and Company, 1990.

Typing

Erickson, Lawrence. Mavis Bacon Teaches Typing: A Brief Course. Mason, OH: South-Western, 2004.

Appendix G

Job Search Resources

Boldt, Arnold G. Resumes for the Rest of Us Secrets from the Pros for Job Seekers with Unconventional Career Paths. Franklin Lakes, NJ: Career Press, 2008.

Enelow, Wendy S., Ronald L. Krannich. Best Resume and Letters for Ex-Offenders. Manassa Park, VA: Impact Publications, 2006.

Jones, Louis N. I Need a J-O-B: The Ex-Offender's Job Search Manual. Washington, D.C.: Conquest Books, 2005.

Krannich, Ronald L. Best Job for Ex-Offenders. Manassas, VA: Impact Publications, 2009.

_____. The Ex-Offender's Job Hunting Guide: 10 Steps to a New Life in the Work World. Manassas Park, VA: Impact Publications, 2005.

_____. No One Will Hire Me: Avoid 15 Mistakes and Win the Job. Manassas Park, VA: Impact Publications, 2007.

Lordan, Kathleen M. The Ex-Offender's Job Search Companion: Getting a Good Job despite Your Record. Lawrenceville, NJ: Cambridge Educational, 2005.

Starting Fresh. Interviewing with a Troubled Background. DVD. Jacksonville, FL: Linx Educational, 2007.

Starting Fresh. Resumes & Cover Letters with a Troubled Background. DVD. Jacksonville, FL: Linx Educational, 2007.

www.ingramcontent.com/pod-product-compliance
Lightning Source LLC
Chambersburg PA
CBHW032015170526
45157CB00002B/706